The Academy of the Poor

Interventions, 2

J. Webb Mealy

General Editors
Robert P. Carroll, David J.A. Clines

The Academy of the Poor

Towards a Dialogical Reading of the Bible

Gerald O. West

Sheffield
Academic Press

Copyright © 1999 Sheffield Academic Press

Published by
Sheffield Academic Press Ltd
Mansion House
19 Kingfield Road
Sheffield S11 9AS
England

Typeset by Sheffield Academic Press
and
Printed on acid-free paper in Great Britain
by Cromwell Press
Trowbridge, Wiltshire

British Library Cataloguing in Publication Data

A catalogue record for this book is available
from the British Library

ISBN 1 85075 758 5

Contents

Acknowledgments

I had thought that I had said most of what is in this book in already published pieces, but the discussions I have had with those who have read and understood and those who have read and misunderstood what I have written have prompted me to write this book. They have probed and pushed me to say more and to say it more clearly and carefully. Thank you to them.

Thank you too to Beverley Haddad, Bafana Khumalo, Tim Long, Sipho Mtetwa, Hilary Mijoga, David Clines and Webb Mealy for reading earlier drafts and offering helpful comments. The final form has benefitted from their attention.

The financial assistance of the Centre for Science Development of the Human Sciences Research Council and the University of Natal Research Fund towards this research is hereby gratefully acknowledged. I am most grateful for the Alexander Robertson Lectureship in the Department of Biblical Studies at the University of Glasgow from April to July 1995 which gave me the opportunity to do preliminary work on the book.

I dedicate this book to Dumisani Phungula, McGlory Speckman, Bafana Khumalo, Malika Sibeko, Sipho Mtetwa and Martin Mandew, organic intellectuals who have made my work possible. *Aluta continua.*

Introduction: Liberation Hermeneutics and Other Matters

The dilemma that confronts black South Africans in their relationship with the Bible is captured in the following well-known anecdote: 'When the white man came to our country he had the Bible and we had the land. The white man said to us "let us pray". After the prayer, the white man had the land and we had the Bible.' This anecdote clearly points to the central position that the Bible occupies in the process of oppression and exploitation. The anecdote also reflects the paradox of the oppressor and the oppressed sharing the same Bible and the same faith. However, what is remarkable about this anecdote is that Desmond Tutu responded to it after one of its tellings by stating, 'And we got the better deal'. While Tutu's response has been challenged, it does capture something of the reality of the Bible in South Africa (and elsewhere): it plays an important role in the lives of many, particularly the poor and marginalized. The Bible is a symbol of the presence of the God of life with them and a resource in their struggle for survival, liberation and life.

This is true of a whole range of readers, including largely illiterate 'readers' from African Independent Churches in the townships and informal shack settlements,[1] militant unionized workers who are active in local civic structures but who are disillusioned with the church,[2] rural black women who not only bear the triple

---

1. G. Philpott, *Jesus Is Tricky and God Is Undemocratic: The Kin-dom of God in Amawoti* (Pietermaritzburg: Cluster Publications, 1993).

2. J.R. Cochrane, 'Already, But Not Yet: Programmatic Notes for a Theology of Work', in J.R. Cochrane and G.O. West, *The Threefold Cord: Theology, Work and Labour* (Pietermaritzburg: Cluster Publications, 1991), pp. 177-89 (181); ICT Church and Labour Project Research Group, 'Workers, the Church and the Alienation of Religious Life', in J.R. Cochrane and G.O.

oppression of race, class and gender, but who also are expected to carry the threefold load, in development terms, of productive, reproductive and community management functions, and who sustain and support the church with their presence, faith and finances,[3] unemployed youth who gave up their education to struggle for liberation and now face an uncertain future, the disabled and unemployable who live on the margins of poor and marginalized communities,[4] and many others. The Bible matters to them.

These are the 'others' who are the subjects of my reflection, those I usually refer to as 'ordinary "readers"'. The term 'reader' alludes to the well-chartered shift in hermeneutics towards the reader.[5] However, I place the term in inverted commas to signal that my use of the term 'reader' is both literal and metaphoric in that it *includes* the many who are illiterate, but who listen to, retell and remake the Bible. The other term in the phrase, the term 'ordinary', is used in a general and a specific sense. The general usage includes all readers who read the Bible pre-critically. But I also use the term 'ordinary' to designate a particular sector of pre-critical readers, those readers who are poor and marginalized. In my discussion the particular usage usually takes precedence over the general.

The other reader who is the subject of my analysis and reection is the socially engaged biblical scholar. Biblical scholars are those

West, *The Threefold Cord: Theology, Work and Labour* (Pietermaritzburg: Cluster Publications, 1991), pp. 253-75 (272).

3.   Beverley Haddad, 'En-gendering a Theology of Development: Raising Some Preliminary Issues', in Leonard Hulley, Louise Kretzschmar and Luke Lungile Pato (eds.), *Archbishop Tutu: Prophetic Witness in South Africa* (Cape Town: Human and Rousseau, 1996), pp. 199-210 (201).

4.   Susan C. Philpott, 'Amawoti: Responding to the Needs and Rights of People with Disabilities' (MSocSc. Thesis: University of Natal, 1995).

5.   M.H. Abrams, *The Mirror and the Lamp: Romantic Theory and the Critical Tradition* (New York: W.W. Norton, 1958), pp. 8-29; John Barton, *Reading the Old Testament: Method in Biblical Study* (London: Darton, Longman & Todd, 1984), pp. 201-207; Bernard C. Lategan, 'Current Issues in the Hermeneutic Debate', *Neotestamentica* 18 (1984), pp. 1-17 (3-4); Edgar V. McKnight, *The Bible and the Reader: An Introduction to Literary Criticism* (Philadelphia: Fortress Press, 1985), pp. 2-3; and Terry Eagleton, 'Reception Theory', in P. Barry (ed.), *Issues in Contemporary Critical Theory* (London: Macmillan, 1989), pp. 119-27 (119).

readers who have been trained in the use of the tools and re-sources of biblical scholarship and who read the Bible 'critically'. So when I use the term 'critical' I do so in the very specific sense that it has within biblical studies. Ordinary readers do have re-sources to read texts critically, but they do not use the structured and systematic sets of resources that constitute the craft of biblical scholars. But my interest is not in biblical scholars in general; I am particularly concerned with those biblical scholars who have cho-sen to collaborate with the poor and marginalized in their strug-gles for survival, liberation and life.

I will say much more about these things in the chapters that fol-low, and so this may be an appropriate point to ask the reader of my book to be patient with me. Because my reading practice, and the reflection and research that emerges from it, includes real, often unruly, 'readers' who do not usually have a place in the cor-ridors of the academy among critical readers of the Bible,[6] much of what I have to say may seem strange and somewhat contro-versial. But as this book is an attempt to give an account of what I and other socially engaged biblical scholars in similar contexts are up to, I do try to analyse as clearly as possible the interpretative processes and products that constitute our work. So please bear with me as you read; the questions you have about what you read may be covered in subsequent pages.

Because socially engaged biblical scholars are already actively engaged in collaborative work of various kinds with poor and marginalized communities, they are often drawn into local Bible reading practices when it is found that they have Bible reading resources. Such has been my repeated experience in the South African context. For example, at the height of the conflict in Kwa-Zulu-Natal during the late 1980s, while I was assisting with the tak-ing of statements and affidavits among a group of people who were refugees from their region, I was asked what kind of work I did. When I said that I taught Biblical Studies at the local univer-sity, they immediately invited me to come and read the Bible with them. Remarkably, this type of invitation is repeated in countless

6.   Stephen D. Moore, 'Doing Gospel Criticism as/with a "Reader"', *Bib-lical Theology Bulletin* 19 (1989), pp. 85-93; see also David Tracy, *Plurality and Ambiguity: Hermeneutics, Religion, Hope* (San Francisco: Harper & Row, 1987), p. 79.

contexts where socially engaged biblical scholars are working with poor and marginalized communities.

This book is an attempt to understand both the invitation and the reading interface that often develops from the invitation, which constitutes the core of liberation hermeneutics. The relationship between socially engaged biblical scholars and ordinary poor and marginalized 'readers' of the Bible lies at the heart of liberation hermeneutics. Liberation theologies in their various forms all emerge from the interface between socially committed biblical scholars and theologians and ordinary Christians from poor and marginalized communities. The task of this book is to understand the contours of the interface more clearly. My particular interest is in the part played by biblical scholars who have responded to the call to go beyond conversation and to collaborate with poor and marginalized readers of the Bible. However, it is inappropriate to analyse this aspect of liberation hermeneutics without some sense of its place within liberation hermeneutics as a whole.

Liberation theologies are quite different from First World Theology (in the singular and with a capital 'T').[7] It is not just that liberation theologies have a different *content*, they are more profoundly different in that they have a different *methodology*. The established methodology of First World theology, often regarded as a universally valid norm, is fundamentally challenged by liberation theologies. While the challenge comes primarily from different quarters in Africa, Asia and Latin America, it also comes from certain sectors within the First World, including labour and women's movements.[8]

Per Frostin, in attempting to describe liberation theologies for his First World colleagues in the academy and church, defines the challenge posed by theologies of liberation with reference to five interrelated emphases: the choice of the interlocutors of theology, the perception of God, the social analysis of conflicts, the choice of theological tools and the relationship between theology

---

7.   Of course there is no one such thing as 'First World Theology', even though proponents would like to think there is. First World theology is really a cluster of theologies with often hidden sets of interests and agendas.

8.   P. Frostin, *Liberation Theology in Tanzania and South Africa: A First World Interpretation* (Lund: Lund University Press, 1988), p. 1.

and praxis.[9] Of particular concern is the first of these emphases, what Frostin calls 'the interlocutors of theology', because it is this emphasis that shapes each of the others.

Frostin notes that all conferences of the Ecumenical Association of Third World Theologians (EATWOT) have argued persistently for a new method of doing theology. The focus of this stress on methodology is expressed in a concern for epistemology. As early as 1976, the founding members of EATWOT declared that this new methodology was based on a 'radical break in epistemology'.

> The theologies from Europe and North America are dominant today in our churches and represent one form of cultural domination. They must be understood to have arisen out of situations related to those countries, and therefore must not be uncritically adopted without our raising the question of their relevance in the context of our countries. Indeed, we must, in order to be faithful to the gospel and to our peoples, reflect on the realities of our own situations and interpret the word of God in relation to these realities. We reject as irrelevant an academic type of theology that is divorced from action. We are prepared for a radical break in epistemology which makes commitment the first act of theology and engages in critical reflection on the praxis of the reality of the Third World.[10]

This quotation makes a number of points, and I will take up many of them in the remainder of the book; however, two points are worth emphasizing at the outset. First, in the methodology of liberation theologies there is a stress on epistemology. When liberation theologians stress the question of epistemology—questions related to the origin, structure, methods and validity of knowledge—they do so in order to insist that their reflection cannot be assessed on the basis of the established epistemology of First World theology. They do not understand their own contribution as a mere reform within an existing framework but as a challenge to a basic consensus.[11]

Second, in the methodology of liberation theologies the experience of oppression and of the struggle for liberation and life are

9.   Frostin, *Liberation Theology in Tanzania*, pp. 6-11.
10.   S. Torres and V. Fabella (eds.), *The Emergent Gospel: Theology from the Underside of History* (Maryknoll, NY: Orbis Books, 1978), p. 269.
11.   Frostin, *Liberation Theology in Tanzania*, pp. 3-4.

fundamental. The opening sentences of one of the first reflections on liberation theologies, Gustavo Gutiérrez's *A Theology of Liberation*, emphasize the role of experience as the starting point for theological reflection:

> This book is an attempt at reflection, based on the Gospel and the experiences of men and women committed to the process of liberation in the oppressed and exploited land of Latin America. It is a theological reflection born of the experience of shared efforts to abolish the current unjust situation to build a different society, freer and more human.[12]

In their emphasis on epistemology and the experience of oppression and the struggle for liberation and life, liberation theologies ask a question not usually asked in Western theology: who are the primary interlocutors of theology? Who are we talking and collaborating with when we read the Bible and do theology? Liberation theologies not only pose this question, they also give a specific answer: the poor and marginalized. Instead of choosing Schleiermacher's 'cultured critics' of religion as its chief interlocutor,[13] liberation theologies have chosen 'nonpersons'—'the poor, the exploited classes, the marginalized races, all the despised cultures'.[14] Furthermore, an option for the poor is more than an ethical choice. Solidarity with the poor also has consequences for the perception of social reality, insisting that the experience of the poor and marginalized is a necessary condition for biblical interpretation and theological reflection. Theologies of liberation require that we not only make 'an option for the poor', but that we also accept 'the epistemological privilege of the poor'.[15] This involves an epistemological paradigm shift in which the poor and marginalized are seen as the primary dialogue partners in reading the Bible and doing theology. Liberation hermeneutics begins

12. G. Gutiérrez, *A Theology of Liberation: History, Politics and Salvation* (London: SCM Press, 1974), p. ix.

13. Cited in Frostin, *Liberation Theology in Tanzania*, p. 6.

14. 'The main issue between progressive Western theology and its interlocutors, has been whether God exists or not, while the central problem in Third World countries is not atheism but an idolatrous submission to systems of oppression' (Frostin, *Liberation Theology in Tanzania*, pp. 7-8).

15. Frostin, *Liberation Theology in Tanzania*, p. 6.

with the reality, experiences, needs, interests, questions and resources of the poor and marginalized.

In the first chapter I demonstrate just what a difference it makes to have the poor and marginalized as our primary interlocutors when we read the Bible. I offer two readings of the same text, one from the First World and one from the South African context. Even the unattentive reader will quickly realize how much my context dominates my discussion. I make no apology for this; this is the context in which I work and which permeates all my analyses and reflections. And I offer my reflections because my studies at Sheffield, the colleagues I encountered there, my travels in various parts of the so-called First World, and the reception of my publications have encouraged me to do so. Much of the material I have used in this book has appeared in other forms elsewhere, but here I attempt to bring together aspects of that work to form a coherent whole. Those who know of my published pieces will recognize repetitions, resonances and shifts. My work tends to be a bit like a battered spider's web, on which I move about enlarging, tinkering, repairing, undoing and remaking. Here I attempt to show the whole, untidy though it may be. This book is, in part, my response to those who have been in dialogue with me, inside and outside of the South African context; in the nicest ways, they have probed and pushed me to explain myself.

In the second chapter I say more about the South African context that has shaped my engagement and scholarship. That the Bible is both a significant and an ambiguous text in the South African context raises serious questions for socially engaged biblical scholars in South Africa, as it does for socially engaged biblical scholars elsewhere. This book, therefore, is my contribution to a wider project in which I see myself collaborating with socially engaged biblical scholars in other contexts. Chapter 2 emphasizes the ethical and epistemological dimensions of my discussion, exploring an ethics of interpretation that includes the voices of the victims of dominant readings of the Bible—those who read the Bible on the boundaries—and calls for a reorientation in Biblical Studies towards the margins. The call remains within the bounds of scholarly discourse, but the reader will at times feel my passion pushing against the limits of scholarly discussion, because in many contexts outside the comfortable corridors of the academy the

Bible is a site of struggle where interpretation is a form of combat and where the effects of our readings are felt and found in flesh and blood.[16]

The thread that runs through Chapter 2 is an analysis of domination and resistance, my argument being that our understanding of the relationship between domination and resistance determines how we understand our role as socially engaged biblical scholars—as intellectuals—in the struggles of the poor and marginalized for survival, liberation and life. My analysis of domination and resistance diminishes the role usually assigned to intellectuals in traditional Marxist accounts.

Asking just what it is that (socially engaged) biblical scholars do is the underlying question throughout Chapter 3. If our role in the struggles of the poor and marginalized is not quite what we had thought, then what is it about what we do that draws the invitations that we regularly receive from ordinary 'readers' of the Bible? As I do throughout the book, I use actual readings as the basic source of my analysis and reflection. Having established what we do when we read the Bible, I then turn in the next chapter, Chapter 4, to explore the contours of the reading practices and resources of ordinary African 'readers' and to probe the place of the socially engaged biblical scholar in relation to these strategies and resources. In order to understand how ordinary Africans 'read' the Bible I adopt both a historical and a methodological perspective, analysing the early encounters between Africans and the Bible in Africa and in North America and the interpretative tools and strategies that have emerged from and were forged by those encounters. This is the longest chapter, and yet the most incomplete in that much more work needs to be done if we are to understand the range of resources ordinary Africans use in their reading practice and so to have some sense of how they might re-envisage the reading practices and place of the socially engaged biblical scholar.

16. I hope there is no need for me to catalogue that this is so. Two recent collections amply demonstrate my point: Fernando F. Segovia and Mary Ann Tolbert (eds.), *Reading from This Place: Social Location and Biblical Interpretation in Global Perspective*, II (Minneapolis: Fortress Press, 1995); and R.S. Sugirthara-jah (ed.), *Voices from the Margin: Interpreting the Bible in the Third World* (Maryknoll, NY: Orbis Books, 1991).

When confronted by assertive and articulate black South Africans in the days of apartheid, white South Africans often said that such black people 'did not know their place'. If my analysis of domination and resistance is appropriate and the poor and marginalized are more assertive and articulate than we imagined, and if they already have substantial reading resources, then what is our place as socially engaged biblical scholars in reading the Bible with them? Do we know our place? This is the question that directs the discussion in Chapter 5. As we have found, we do have a place, but it is perhaps not the place we had imagined!

Chapter 6 offers readers an opportunity to participate in a simulated contextual Bible study—a Bible study in which the respective subject positions of ordinary, untrained 'readers' and critical, trained readers are vigilantly foregrounded and in which power relations are structurally acknowledged. Within the limits of such an exercise readers of this book can get a feel for the process. Viewing the reading process and the reading produced by this process from the perspective of a participant will generate other questions and concerns, many of which will hopefully be addressed in the course of the chapter. Chapter 7 continues the exercise, but this time invites the reader to observe a contextual Bible study through the transcript of an actual Bible study that took place in an informal settlement not far from where I live and teach. Here the readers are left alone to navigate the transcript as they will and make of it what they will.

The concluding chapter, Chapter 8, reads a biblical text with a marginal character in that text and with poor and marginalized communities in the South African context. My reflections on this reading provide a form of summary and conclusion to the book.

What roles do biblical studies and biblical scholars play in those contexts where the Bible is a significant text within poor and marginalized communities? This is the guiding question that weaves its way through each chapter. In addressing this question I draw on liberation hermeneutics (with a focus on race, class and gender), inculturation hermeneutics (with a focus on culture), and postmodernism (with a decentred 'focus'!). I also draw on more familiar resources, showing that recent trends in the field of biblical studies open up space for serious dialogue—even collaboration—between readers of the Bible in the academy and 'readers' of the Bible in poor and marginalized communities.

The story I began with in which Desmond Tutu recounts the Bible's presence among us is a part of the larger narrative of the reading of the Bible in South Africa, where the Bible is a significant text which has shaped and will continue to shape our history. The story of the Bible in South Africa remains complex and ambiguous: for most of the people in South Africa, the majority of whom are Christian, the Bible has been both oppressor and liberator; it has supported apartheid and struggled against apartheid; it stands against them and it stands with them.

Even now, after our first democratic elections, the inauguration of Nelson Mandela as our President, and the establishment of a government of national unity popularly elected by the people, the ambiguity of the Bible remains, presenting itself in different forms as our context shifts and changes. *The Kairos Document,* which emerged from the struggle against apartheid more than ten years ago, argued that 'the crisis' in South Africa 'impels us *to return to the Bible* and to search the Word of God for a message that is relevant to what we are experiencing in South Africa today'.[17] In other words, the crisis that was shaking the foundations of our country was both political and interpretative. Wonderfully, we are emerging from our political crisis with a popularly elected democratic government, though, as the daily sittings of the Truth and Reconciliation Commission declare, the dismantling of apartheid and the healing of its damage is painful and protracted. Unfortunately, however, our interpretative crisis is deepening.

The Kairos Document was, as its subtitle intended, a 'challenge to the church', as was the document produced a few years later, *The Road to Damascus: Kairos and Conversion.*[18] Sectors of the church responded to these challenges, joining those who already were engaged in various ways in the struggle against apartheid. The church (like the synagogue, mosque and temple) became a site of struggle. However, now that our political crisis has passed, there are worrying indications that, in the words of a prominent churchman, 'the church must now go back to being the church'. But

17. *The Kairos Document: Challenge to the Church* (Braamfontein: Skotaville, 1986), p. 17.

18. *The Road to Damascus: Kairos and Conversion* (Johannesburg: Skotaville, 1989).

surely we were most truly 'church' in the streets of our struggle? While it is no longer necessary for the church to represent the liberation movements, as it was in decades of their bannings, this does not mean that the readings and theologies forged in the struggle ought to be abandoned in order to 'go back to being the church', whatever this might mean.

Our struggle *against* apartheid demanded new readings and theologies of us. Our struggle *for* full liberation and life requires that we build on what we have learned. The present danger is that we do indeed 'go back to being the church', even before we have adequately articulated the readings and theologies which we lived by in the days of struggle and which will enable us to go forward to full liberation and life. The 'working' readings and theologies that resourced our struggle, and that many who struggle to survive each day still live by, are in danger of being forgotten as the church sighs and begins to pick up the patterns of the past. This is our deepening interpretative crisis.

Political liberation in South Africa has created some 'space' for the church, but just how that space is to be filled is a crucial question. Now is not the time to return to comfortable certainties, rather now is the time for the recognition and articulation of the subjugated and incipient resources of our struggle. Subjugated and incipient readings of the Bible and their related theologies have been resources for many, particularly for the poor and marginalized, and their struggle for survival, liberation and life is not yet over.

1 |

The Difference it Makes
with Whom We Read

In a recent encyclical letter, *Veritatis Splendor* (August 1993), Pope
John Paul II offers a reading of the story of the rich young man in
Matthew's Gospel (Mt. 19.16-26). The Pope's interpretation, produced in a process which is not yet readily apparent,[1] views this
story as 'a useful guide' to the moral teaching of Jesus.[2] The question that the rich young man brings to Jesus is a question about
morality, '*about the full meaning of life*' (7). In this unnamed rich
young man 'we can recognize every person' who approaches Jesus
and questions him about morality (7).

I will not summarize the Pope's reading in detail, but I do want
to draw attention to some features of this reading, because this is
a reading that matters—it has effects. The reading of John Paul II
follows the contours of the text quite closely, but also regularly
reads this text through a range of intertexts, both biblical and
ecclesiastical. Allusions are also made to the broad socio-historical
background of the story, but not in detail. So, for example, it is
noted that the rich young man is 'a devout Israelite, raised in the
shadow of the Law', and that therefore in asking Jesus 'Teacher,
what good must I do to have eternal life' (Mt. 19.16), he is probably not ignorant of the answer contained in the Law, but rather

---

1.   In his introduction to a volume of comments and analysis on *Veritatis
Splendor*, John Wilkins notes that the history of production of this encyclical
will one day be visible 'and will throw light on the debates that went into its
production and the winners and losers in that process' (John Wilkins, 'Introduction', in J. Wilkins [ed.], *Understanding Veritatis Splendor: The Encyclical
Letter of Pope John Paul II on the Church's Moral Teaching* [London: SPCK,
1994], p. ix).

2.   *Veritatis Splendor*, para. 6. All further paragraph references to this text
will be placed in brackets at the end of a quote.

is prompted by 'the attractiveness of the person of Jesus' to ask a new question about the moral good (8). However, the dominant mode of reading is that of following the text fairly closely.

This quite careful reading of the text centres on the narrative exchanges between the characters. In asking his question, the rich young man 'senses that there is a connection between moral good and the fulfillment of his own destiny' (8). The initial part of the response of Jesus, 'There is only one who is good', reminds the rich young man that only God can answer the question because goodness 'has its source in God', and indeed that God is the Good (9). The second part of the response, 'If you wish to enter into life, keep the commandments', makes a second connection, this time between eternal life and obedience to God's command-ments: God's commandments show 'the path of life and they lead to it' (12).

But Jesus' answer 'is not enough for the young man'; he probes further by asking which commandments must be kept. Having directed 'the young man's gaze towards God', now 'Jesus reminds him of the commandments of the Decalogue regarding one's neighbour' (13). John Paul II quickly adds, however, that 'From the context of the conversation, and especially a comparison of Matthew's text with the parallel passages in Mark and Luke', the emphasis here is not on 'each and every one of the command-ments' but on the 'centrality' of the Decalogue (13). 'Neverthe-less we cannot fail to notice which commandments of the Law the Lord recalls to the young man' (13). They are the command-ments to do with the love of neighbour, with the 'dignity of the human person'. 'The commandments of which Jesus reminds the young man are meant to safeguard *the good* of the person, the image of God, by protecting his [*sic*] *goods*'. 'These negative pre-cepts express with particular force the ever urgent need to protect human life, the communion of persons in marriage, private prop-erty, truthfulness and people's good name' (13). They are also 'the *first necessary step on the journey towards freedom*, its starting point' (13).

The answer the rich young man receives concerning the com-mandments, notes the Pope, 'does not satisfy the young man', who takes the conversation further by asking Jesus another ques-tion: 'I have kept all these; what do I still lack?' (Mt. 19.20). The reading then grapples at length with these two sentences: the statement and the question. John Paul II states that it 'is not easy to say with a clear conscience "I have kept all these", if one has any understanding of the demands contained in God's Law' (16). 'And yet', he continues, 'even though he is able to make this reply, even though he has followed the moral ideal seriously and generously from childhood, the rich young man knows that he is still lacking something' (16). 'Conscious of *the young man's yearning for something greater, which would transcend a legalistic interpretation of the commandments*, the Good Teacher invites him to enter upon the path of perfection: "If you wish to be perfect, go, sell your possessions and give the money to the poor, and you will have treasure in heaven; then come, follow me" (Mt. 19.21).'

The Pope then immediately points out that 'Like the earlier part of Jesus' answer, this part too must be read and interpreted in the context of the whole moral message of the Gospel, and in particular in the context of the Sermon on the Mount, the Beatitudes (cf. Mt. 5.3-12), the first of which is precisely the Beatitude of the poor, the "poor in spirit", as Saint Matthew makes clear (Mt. 5.3), the humble' (16). Quite how the reading moves from this point is not clear, because here there is no careful conversation with the text. The next time this part of the text appears we read that

> This vocation to perfect love is not restricted to a small group of individuals. *The invitation*, 'go, sell your possessions and give the money to the poor', and the promise 'you will have treasure in heaven', *are meant for everyone*, because they bring out the full meaning of the commandment of love for neighbour, just as the invitation which follows, 'Come, follow me', is the new, specific form of the commandment of love of God' (18). Both the commandments and Jesus' invitation to the rich young man stand at the service of a single and indivisible charity, which spontaneously tends towards that perfection whose measure is God alone…(18).

Here, it seems to me, text is abandoned for other intertexts which lead away from conversation with this text. Having quite carefully read the contours of the text up to this place, the reading now follows another path.

> The way and at the same time the content of this perfection consist in the following of Jesus, *sequela Christi*, once one has given up one's own wealth and very self. This is precisely the conclusion of

> Jesus' conversation with the young man: 'Come, follow me' (Mt.
> 19.21). It is an invitation the marvellous grandeur of which will be
> fully perceived by the disciples after Christ's Resurrection, when
> the Holy Spirit leads them to all truth (cf. Jn 16.13) (19).

This is the only mention of wealth in the entire reading, and the
actual poor are never present, not even when the reading follows
the story through to Jesus' challenge to his disciples. In the text
(Mt. 19.23-26) Jesus says to his disciples, 'I tell you solemnly, it will
be hard for a rich man to enter the kingdom of heaven. Yes, I tell
you again, it is easier for a camel to pass through the eye of a
needle than for a rich man to enter the kingdom of heaven' (Mt.
19.23-24; JB). Pope John Paul II ignores these verses entirely by a
remarkable slight of hand:

> The conclusion of Jesus' conversation with the rich young man is
> very poignant: 'When the young man heard this, he went away
> sorrowful, for he had many possessions' (Mt. 19.22). Not only the
> rich man but the disciples themselves are taken aback by Jesus' call
> to discipleship, the demands of which transcend human aspira-
> tions and abilities: 'When the disciples heard this, they were greatly
> astounded and said, "Then who can be saved?" (Mt. 19.25). *But the
> Master refers them to God's power.* "With men this is impossible, but
> with God all things are possible"' (Mt. 19.26) (22).

The disciples' response, of course, is not only to Jesus' challenge to the rich young man, but also to his challenge to them in
vv. 23-24, the verses that are elided in this reading.

Readers, even ordinary untrained readers, who read the text for
themselves will notice this gap. The Pope's reading goes on as if
this gap did not exist, speaking of love, grace, God's power, freedom, truth and morality. It is true, as John Paul II asserts in his
concluding section, that 'Jesus' conversation with the rich young
man continues, in a sense, *in every period of history, including our
own*' (25). But for most of us this conversation includes questions
of wealth and poverty, the rich and the poor, so clearly present in
the text. The gap left by the Pope's reading remains a gap, an
absence that must be interpreted. We cannot, you see, talk of love,
grace, God's power, freedom, truth and morality without speaking
of these absent things.

Jesus' conversation with the rich young man continues in South
Africa today, but it is rather different from its form in *Veritatis*

Splendor. Below I record readings of this story in South African contexts, outlining both the reading process and product.

In a research project with a range of Anglican Bible study groups in Pietermaritzburg, South Africa, a colleague and I noted that almost all the readers, irrespective of their different contexts, understood Mk 10.17-22 (the parallel passage of Mt. 19.16-26) as a story about individual sin.[3] According to them, in this story the sin was putting wealth/possessions before following Jesus. This was the sin of the man in the story (in the time of Jesus), and this was a potential sin for present day readers. The challenge to the wealthy man (then) and to the participants (now) was to make sure that wealth was not an idol, that possessions did not come between them and Jesus.

In one or two groups, significantly groups from poor and marginalized communities, there was some discussion of 'structural sin'. In other words, participants in some groups argued that the problem was not only one of individual sin but also one of structural or systemic sin. However, only one group pursued this reading with any persistence.[4] But it was this possible reading which provoked a series of Bible studies, particularly as 'structural sin' was a key concept at that time in the struggle against apartheid.[5] A series of workshops which I was subsequently invited to facilitate provided a useful opportunity to develop a contextual Bible study on Mk 10.17-22.

Briefly, what has come to be called 'contextual Bible study' in South Africa is a Bible reading process that takes place within the framework of liberation hermeneutics. The framework of commitments that encompasses contextual Bible study include: first, a commitment to begin the reading process from the experienced reality of the organized poor and marginalized, including their language, categories, concepts, needs, questions, interests and resources; second, a commitment to read the Bible communally 'with' each other, where power relations are acknowledged and

3. Jonathan A. Draper and Gerald O. West, 'Anglicans and Scripture in South Africa', in Frank England and Torquil J.M. Paterson (eds.), *Bounty in Bondage* (Johannesburg: Ravan, 1989), pp. 30-52 (42-43).

4. Draper and West, 'Anglicans and Scripture', p. 43.

5. A. Nolan, *God in South Africa: The Challenge of the Gospel* (Cape Town: David Philip, 1988); *The Kairos Document.*

equalized as far as possible; third, a commitment to read the Bible critically, using whatever critical resources are available, including local critical resources and the critical resources of biblical scholarship; and fourth, a commitment to social transformation through the Bible reading process.

The Bible studies were conducted during seven workshops with people from a number of different contexts, the majority of whom were from poor and marginalized communities. A common feature of all workshops was that most of the participants were politically conscientized. For each of the groups the Bible was a significant text and Bible study a serious religious experience. There was considerable continuity between workshops in that my own contribution to a particular workshop had been shaped extensively by the previous workshop(s). In addition, I would also share the comments and questions of the participants in previous workshops with those in subsequent workshops. This enabled a form of represented dialogue to develop between successive workshops.

My commitment to reading 'with' the participants,[6] rather than reading 'for' them, required that I acknowledge and foreground my own contribution to the reading process, which was limited to constantly encouraging and facilitating a close and careful reading of the text. The substantive contribution came from the resources, categories, concepts and experiences of ordinary readers. Nevertheless, in each workshop I was acutely aware of the power dynamics implicit in my presence. My academic biblical training gave me power in the context of Bible study, as did my whiteness and maleness. While I recognize that there are always multifarious points of power,[7] and while I was often aware of other locations of power in the group, I do not want to minimize my own presence and resources.

I was especially concerned that ordinary readers did not simply defer to my reading/interpretation, that they did not only offer the 'expected', 'orthodox' reading, and that they did not opt for

6. I place considerable weight on the preposition 'with', which I will explain more fully in the following chapter.

7. Michel Foucault, *Power/Knowledge: Selected Writings and Other Interviews* (New York: Pantheon, 1980); see also Sharon Welch, *Communities of Resistance and Solidarity: A Feminist Theology of Liberation* (Maryknoll, NY: Orbis Books, 1985).

'a fundamentalism of the Left' in which the text became simply a site for any meaning that might be required by a particular agenda. I therefore concentrated on posing a series of questions that kept the focus of the reading process on the text, enabling a close and careful reading of the text.[8] When I participated in the discussion I focused my contribution on certain aspects of the text, specifically the link between the commandments (v. 19) and the link between these commandments and the command to the man to sell all that he possesses and to give to the poor (v. 21). Because ordinary readers tend not to read the text carefully and closely,[9] one of my roles as a facilitator was to constantly return their reading to the text. As indicated, I did this primarily by providing the following questions:[10]

1. *General questions*
   (a) What do you think this story meant in the time of Jesus?
   (b) What do you think this story means for us today?

   The following questions may help you to answer these two general questions:

2. *The wealthy man*
   (a) What do we know about this man who spoke to Jesus?
   (b) What do you think he did for a living?
   (c) Why do you think he owned many possessions?
   (d) Why do you think he spoke to Jesus?

3. *The commandments*
   (a) Why do you think Jesus talked about the commandments?
   (b) Why do you think Jesus used these particular commandments?
   (c) What do you think the commandments that Jesus used have in common?
   (d) Why do you think keeping these commandments was not enough to gain eternal life?

---

8. Gerald O. West, 'The Relationship between Different Modes of Reading and the Ordinary Reader', *Scriptura* S9 (1991), pp. 87-110.

9. Draper and West, 'Anglicans and Scripture', pp. 41, 45.

10. This is an abbreviated and slightly adapted form of the Bible study used in Draper and West, 'Anglicans and Scripture'.

(e) Which do you think is more important to Jesus, to keep the commandments or to give to the poor?

4. *The challenge*
    (a) Why do you think Jesus told the man to sell his possessions and give to the poor?
    (b) What do you think the link is between the commandments and the challenge to the man?
    (c) Why do you think Jesus told the man to do this before he could follow him?
    (d) Why do you think the young man did not obey Jesus?
    (e) What do you think Jesus meant by 'treasure in heaven'?

5. *The poor*
    (a) Who do you think Jesus meant by 'the poor' in this story?
    (b) Why do you think they were poor?

6. *Today*
    (a) Does this story say anything to us today?
    (b) Who do you think are similar to the wealthy man today?
    (c) Why do you think they are wealthy?
    (d) Who do you think are the poor today?
    (e) Why do you think they are poor?
    (f) What do you think Jesus' challenge means to us?

The questions generated a range of contributions from the participants. For example, when the readers in these workshops read v. 19 carefully, prompted by the questions on the commandments (see above), there was general agreement that these commandments were concerned with social relationships (in contrast to the omitted commandments which referred to the human-to-God relationship). Once participants realized this, they then began to explore *why* Jesus chose these commandments, and concluded that there was obviously something amiss in the area of the man's social relationships. This realization in turn led to considerable discussion and debate as the readers probed for a more precise understanding of the problems in this person's social relationships.

As the readers began to explore and probe these questions, they were constantly driven to reread the text. For example, many readers moved back and forth between the questions concerning the challenge of Jesus and the text, returning to the text again and again to reread it more closely and carefully. Verse 22, with its reference to 'much property',[11] became a key verse in their attempt to understand this man's wealth.

The more critical reading process encouraged by the questions provided did not prevent readers from drawing on their own experience and resources. Their rereading of the text generated at first a certain amount of frustration, because the text did not seem to give many clues concerning the man's social relationships. However, by drawing on their own South African experience some readers argued that the man probably obtained his 'much property' through exploiting others. There were other readers who argued that this was not the only possible reading, and that this man could have worked hard for or inherited his 'much property'. Through most of this discussion and debate I attempted to facilitate discussion on as broad a basis as possible, encouraging all participants to share their views. But as I have already stated, my main contribution was to pose specific questions which would return readers to the text, which I did by focusing their reading on the textual relationship between the commandments (v. 19), the command to the man to sell all he possessed and to give to the poor (v. 21), and the statement that he owned much property (v. 22), encouraging them to explore the internal relationships within the text.

As they delved into the text more deeply, those readers who had argued that the man had probably obtained his 'much property' by exploiting others, based on their own South African experience, now found textual evidence to support this argument. Gradually others began to see this argument, and so a reading of Mk 10.17-22 which included a concern for social and structural sin began to emerge (see below).

(In the last workshop in the series I also offered 'external' socio-historical resources into the reading process at the request of the participants, providing them with some sense of the socio-historical context that produced the text. My socio-historical sketch of first-century Palestine included the sociology of the Jesus

---

11. No one translation was used during these Bible studies. Participants used various translations in various languages. I am using the New American Standard translation here and below.

movement, the temple-state system[12] and other historical and sociological factors which interested the participants and which
assisted their understanding of Mk 10.17-22.)

In terms of process, then, my contribution focused on facilitating a close reading of the text. (In one case I provided some
socio-historical resources.) With my contribution and their own
considerable resources we came to the following reading of Mk
10.17-22. Along with many other ordinary readers,[13] the participants in these workshops understood this text to be about individual sin, the sin of making wealth and possessions an idol, and of
allowing wealth and possessions to come between people and
God. But the ordinary readers who participated in the workshops
also understood this text to be about social and structural sin.

In exploring the relationship between the commandments
(v. 19), the command to the man to sell all he possessed and to
give to the poor (v. 21), and the statement that he owned much
property (v. 22), we understood that the text (and Jesus)[14] made a
connection between the socially orientated commandments, the
wealth of the man, and the poor. We argued that Jesus chose
these commandments because he knew that the man had gained
his 'much property' by exploiting the poor, whether or not the
man himself had done so consciously or personally. In other
words, we argued that there might have been social structures
which produced wealth for the man and exploited the people, in
the same way that the social system of apartheid empowered white
South Africans to become wealthy and pushed black South Africans into poverty. So even if the man had worked hard for his

12. My sociological sketch was based substantially on the work of the fol-
lowing scholars: Richard A. Horsley, *Sociology and the Jesus Movement* (New
York: Crossroad, 1989); Herman C. Waetjen, *A Reordering of Power: A Socio-
Political Reading of Mark's Gospel* (Minneapolis: Fortress Press, 1989); Klaus
Wengst, *Pax Romana and the Peace of Jesus Christ* (London: SCM Press, 1987);
Albert Nolan, *Jesus before Christianity: The Gospel of Liberation* (Cape Town:
David Philip, 1986).

13. See Draper and West, 'Anglicans and Scripture', pp. 42-43.

14. Ordinary readers did not distinguish between 'the text' and 'Jesus'.
The ideological perspective of this particular text was not the concern of
these Bible studies, although some participants did raise the question when
referring to the synoptic parallels (see also Draper and West, 'Anglicans and
Scripture', p. 41).

property or had inherited his wealth, he was still part of sinful social structures.

Given this reading, the challenge of Jesus to the man (v. 21) to sell all he possessed and to give to the poor made sense. The man could not follow Jesus until he had repented of, and made restitution for, his participation in social and structural sin. As the Third World document *The Road to Damascus* argues,[15] some participants noted, following Jesus requires structural repentance and conversion.

(My introduction of socio-historical background information in the final workshop contributed to this understanding. Recognizing that Jesus was from among the poor, and that the early Jesus movement consisted largely of the poor, made it even clearer why the man must first sell all he possessed and give to the poor. The man could not participate in a sinful system and participate in the Jesus movement. He had to make a choice.)

The commandments in v. 19 also took on a new meaning in the light of this reading. The man thought that he had kept the commandments, but he was thinking only on an individual level. While he himself might not have murdered anyone, or committed adultery, or stolen, or given false testimony, or defrauded, or dishonoured his parents, he was a part of, and perpetuated, a system that did all of these things. The ordinary readers in the workshops, most of whom were black, gave countless examples of how the apartheid system had resulted in murder, adultery, theft, legal injustice, unjust wages and the destruction of black family life. For example, an inadequate health system for black people, impoverished 'homelands' and townships, and biased and brutal security forces murdered black people every day. The migrant labour system, pass laws, the group areas act, and single-sex hostels all generated adultery and destroyed family life. Forced removals, no minimum wage, and education for inferiority were forms of theft and fraud. The discriminatory legal system and the state-controlled media constantly disseminated false and biased testimony.

(The readers in the final workshop were fascinated by the socio-historical world of Palestine in the time of Jesus, and immediately

15. *The Road to Damascus.* This document was produced by Third World Christians from South Africa, Namibia, South Korea, Philippines, El Salvador, Nicaragua and Guatemala.

saw South African parallels with the temple-state system, Roman occupation, ruling 'class' Jewish–Roman collaboration, the Sanhedrin, landowners, day-labourers, peasants, the position of women, etc. While I consistently cautioned against simple correspondences between 'then' and 'now',[16] this socio-historical perspective was clearly useful to the ordinary readers and provided additional resources for their reading of the text.)

The challenge of Mk 10.17-22 was clear to us. The man, and those who are like him today, must repent and make restitution before they/we could be reconciled to God. This text (and Jesus) seemed to say that there could be not reconciliation with God, and no membership in the community of Jesus, without repentance and restitution. So while we must be constantly alert to wealth as an idolatrous danger, we must also be constantly critical of our social location in sinful structures and systems.

I have presented two readings of a biblical text. I have not tried to be neutral; my interests, both interpretative and social, are fairly clear, and will become even clearer in the chapters that follow. However, I have tried to present two readings without too much analysis and commentary. That is really the task of subsequent chapters. I have resisted footnotes at the many points where my account cries out for them, hoping that the unfinished feel draws the reader to read on and delve with me as I take up these points in subsequent chapters. I have also tried to be honest in portraying my own work, though my perspective and approach have shifted somewhat since those Bible studies in the late 1980s and early 1990s. The nature of my shifts will also become apparent in what follows.

While this chapter offers readers a useful feel of and for my context, work and reflection, my main purpose in this chapter has been to demonstrate the difference it makes whom we read with. The significant difference between these readings is who the primary interlocutors are; the Pope has chosen to read with other trained—scholarly—readers in a place of privilege and power, whereas I have chosen to read with ordinary African readers in

16. Clodovis Boff, *Theology and Praxis: Epistemological Foundations* (Maryknoll, NY: Orbis Books, 1987), pp. 132-53; Jonathan A. Draper, ' "Go Sell All You Have…" (Mark 10.17-30)', *Journal of Theology for Southern Africa* 79 (1992), pp. 63-69 (67); Nolan, *God in South Africa*, pp. 7-30.

places of poverty and marginalization. The significant similarity between these readings is that they are both readings that matter; both these readings will have effects in and on the lives of people. For those of us who work in contexts where readings of the Bible matter, whom we choose to read with makes a difference that matters. How we read with those we have chosen to read with also makes a difference that matters. To this we now turn.

2 |

Reading with: A Call to Conversion

During the latter half of the 1980s KwaZulu-Natal was at war. The United Democratic Front (UDF), a popular anti-apartheid coalition launched in 1983, was rapidly gaining support, organizing and mobilizing throughout South Africa. With a mandate from the banned African National Congress (ANC), extensive affiliation by a variety of community-based organizations, including sectors of the church, and strong and enabling local leadership, the UDF gained substantial grassroots support. However, in Kwa-Zulu-Natal the growth of the UDF was not only opposed and obstructed by the state, as elsewhere, but also by Inkatha, then a so-called cultural organization, but also the puppet party used by its apartheid masters in Pretoria to administer a so-called Zulu 'homeland', who consider KwaZulu-Natal their traditional 'tribal' territory.

Inkatha responded to the UDF's growing support by embarking on an intimidating membership drive, particularly in those areas where the UDF was beginning to set up structures.[1] Whenever and wherever people resisted being press-ganged into Inkatha membership violence followed.[2] Funded, trained, armed, transported and supported by the apartheid state, Inkatha attempted to crush the UDF.[3] The violence this has generated is horrific and every black family in the region has experienced terror and death.

---

1.   In the post-apartheid era the UDF has dissolved and Inkatha has transformed itself into a fully fledged political party, the Inkatha Freedom Party (IFP).

2.   This was the so-called 'black on black violence' popularized by ignorant international media, and makes as much sense as speaking of the conflict in Bosnia as 'white on white violence'.

3.   Ann Truluck, *No Blood on our Hands* (Pietermaritzburg: Black Sash, 1993).

One of the many cries to emerge from the violence was, as *The Kairos Document* demonstrates, a cry to reread the Bible in such a way as to discover the God of life in the midst of the forces of death. Received readings and theologies no longer made sense. The biblical and theological resources for those struggling with the God of life against the forces of death were not always apparent. Remarkably, this questioning brought Bible 'readers' from poor and marginalized communities into dialogue with socially engaged biblical scholars at the university. The struggle for survival, liberation and life was ecumenical,[4] including those in the Settler Initiated Churches (Catholic, Anglican, Methodist, Presbyterian, etc.) as well as the thousands of African Initiated/Independent Churches (Zionist, Shembe, Ethiopian, etc.) in which belonging, identity, healing, mutual support, communal integration and survival are the primary concerns.[5] Ours is a context in which biblical interpretations do matter; they do shape our world. As the South African context constantly reminds us, biblical interpretations have life and death consequences; they shape the type of response the state, the church, and ordinary people make to particular social realities. They have effects.

Our initial response as biblical scholars to the dialogue was an overwhelming sense of the inadequacy and paucity of our resources in this context. And yet the call of the community also helped us to recognize that we did have resources which might be useful, provided we were willing to read the Bible and do theology 'with' them. The result of our dialogue, as I indicated earlier, is an emerging interface in which socially engaged biblical scholars and poor and marginalized 'readers' of the Bible do what we call 'contextual Bible study'—a form of Bible reading that begins with an emancipatory interest that is grounded in the real conditions of poor and marginalized local communities.

As I briefly described in the Introduction, the beginnings of such collaboration are found in the encounters between biblical scholars and ordinary 'readers' of the Bible in poor and marginalized communities as they work together, often on projects not

4. This was also true in an even broader 'ecumenical' sense, and included those among the poor and marginalized from other faiths and no faith.

5. See James R. Cochrane, 'Circles of Dignity: Incipient Theologies and the Integrity of Faith in a Postcolonial Era' (unpublished manuscript), p. 81.

directly related to the Bible. Collaborative Bible reading arises from other forms of social collaboration. For biblical scholars who do not come from poor and marginalized communities becoming socially engaged requires some form of conversion. The forms our conversions take are as different as our identities and contexts.

My own process of conversion is rooted in my white, middle-class, male and Christian identity and the South African context. White, middle-class males are groomed for greatness, particularly in the apartheid past of South Africa. We grow up expecting to be major players in the scheme of things. And even if we partially betray our race, class and gender by struggling against apartheid and its legacy we still expect to play a pivotal role in that struggle. It was only when I briefly left South Africa in the mid-1980s to study in Sheffield, just as a State of Emergency had been declared, and spent time with black exiles, that my perspective and expectations were changed. Black South African exiles made two things abundantly clear to me. They made it clear that they were in no doubt that I should return to South Africa, because that was where I belonged; they could not, in fact, understand that there might be any other option. Their own experience of living in England was that of exile, and they simply assumed that this was my experience as well. But they also made it clear what my role on my return ought to be. Greatness was not my destiny; others would soon fulfil that role, and they would not be white. And yet, my black comrades maintained, I did having something to offer in our struggle for survival, liberation and life. The resources and skills that I had obtained through my position of privilege, and at the cost of their oppression, should be made available to the struggle. I had a role, but the role was to wait for the call to serve, and then to serve.

My black comrades in exile then, and many other black colleagues, friends and communities since, have asked me to make myself of use to them. I am still learning what it means 'to be made use of', and I am discovering in the process that I am becoming partially constituted by my work with them. Work with poor and marginalized communities enables white, middle-class, male biblical scholars like me to be constituted partially by the experiences, needs, questions and resources of such communities. This does not mean that my 'whiteness', 'middle-classness' and 'maleness' cease to be the major factors that constitute me, but they are no longer the whole story. I will need to be reminded again and again that I am indeed substantially shaped and indelibly inscribed by my whiteness, middle-classness and maleness, but I now know that I need not remain content to always be so.

In attempting to be made use of I, like others in my situation, have discovered that 'conversion from below' is an ongoing process with multiple dimensions. The initial phase of conversion—forms of social engagement with the poor and marginalized—in contexts where the Bible is a significant text often leads to biblical scholars being invited to participate in Bible reading with local communities. The invitation to participate brings with it other dimensions of conversion. Our experience in South Africa, and the experience of colleagues in similar contexts, for example in Brazil, has demonstrated two potential problems which constantly recur when biblical scholars participate in Bible reading with local communities of the poor and marginalized: biblical scholars either romanticize and idealize the contribution of the poor and marginalized or they minimize and rationalize that community's contribution. Both an uncritical 'listening to', that romanticizes and idealizes the interpretations of the poor and marginalized, and an arrogant 'speaking for', that minimizes and rationalizes the interpretations of the poor and marginalized, must be problematized.

But in order to problematize these different positions we must understand something of the analysis that generates each of them. As I have indicated in my Introduction, at the heart of liberation hermeneutics is the relationship between the biblical scholar (or theologian) and the ordinary Christian 'reader' from a poor and marginalized community. We must now probe the form of that relationship more carefully.

There are two analytical trajectories with respect to this relationship. In the Latin American context Jan Luis Segundo describes each trajectory with remarkable clarity, delineating the shift within Latin American theology between what he calls 'two lines' of analysis within liberation theology. The one line of analysis emphasizes the categories and contribution of the theologian or biblical scholar, while the other foregrounds the categories and contribution of 'the common people'.

Segundo looks at the history, aims, methods, and results of these two co-existing lines of analysis in Latin America. The first line of analysis has three characteristics: the solidarity of biblical scholars and theologians with the poor and marginalized, a methodological suspicion that Christian faith at all levels of society is ideologically distorted and thus serves the status quo, and finally, a commitment to provide 'the pastoral activities of the Church with a new and de-ideologized theology capable of speaking about the common themes of Christian faith'.[6] Because it is the social sciences that 'provide the theologian who wants to carry out a de-ideologizing task with valuable cognitive tools', and because these are 'tools which…are beyond the grasp of the majority of people',[7] the role of the theologian or biblical scholar is emphasized. An option is made for the poor, but the categories and contribution of their experience are subordinated to, or translated into, the terms of the intellectual trained in the social sciences.

However, Segundo shows that the rise of popular movements either outside or inside the church 'had shown that common people had neither understood nor welcomed anything from the first theology of liberation, and had actually reacted against its criticism of the supposed oppressive elements of popular religion'.[8] It became clear, therefore, that 'if theologians were still to be the "organic intellectuals" of the common people, that is to say useful as intellectuals charged with the understanding of popular faith, they were obliged to learn how oppressed people lived their faith'.[9] So theologians wanting to be in religious matters the organic intellectuals of poor and marginalized people, 'began then to understand their function as one of unifying and structuring people's understanding of their faith, as well as grounding and defending the practices coming from this faith'.[10] Here the categories and concepts of the poor and marginalized are foregrounded.

---

6. J.L. Segundo, 'The Shift within Latin American Theology', *Journal of Theology for Southern Africa* 52 (1985), pp. 17-29 (22).
7. Segundo, 'The Shift', p. 28.
8. Segundo, 'The Shift', p. 23.
9. Segundo, 'The Shift', p. 23.
10. Segundo, 'The Shift', p. 24.

The tension between these two positions can be found in every context in which there is a struggle for survival, liberation and life, and at the centre of the tension, as I have already suggested, is the different understanding of relationship between the socially engaged biblical scholar or theologian and the ordinary poor and marginalized believer. The emphasis tends to be either on the critical contribution of the trained reader or on the reading resources of the ordinary 'reader'. Although Segundo, like many other liberation theologians, empathizes with much in this latter line of analysis, he is reluctant to give up the *critical* function inherent in the first line of analysis. The reason for his reluctance lies in his understanding of the dynamics of oppression and domination and in the role of the (organic) intellectual in resisting oppression and domination.

Informed by forms of Marxist analysis and aspects of our experience, many of us, including Segundo, believed that forms of critical consciousness are necessary so that the poor and marginalized can 'create their own language'.[11] Forms of critical consciousness, we argued, break 'the culture of silence' created by the accommodation of the poor and marginalized to the logic of domination. This was certainly my own understanding in the early days of my work with local communities of the poor and marginalized in South Africa. But now I am not so sure that this understanding is the whole story.

When it comes to understanding the alleged silence of the poor and marginalized we find thick and thin accounts of ideological hegemony. The thick version emphasizes the role of ideological state apparatuses, such as education systems, the church and government structures, in controlling the symbolic means of production, just as factory owners monopolize the material means of production. 'Their ideological work secures the active consent of subordinate groups to the social arrangements that reproduce their subordination.'[12] The thin theory of hegemony makes less grand claims for the ideological control of the ruling class. What ideological domination does accomplish, according to this version,

11. Frostin, *Liberation Theology in Tanzania*, p. 10.

12. James C. Scott, *Domination and the Arts of Resistance: Hidden Transcipts* (New Haven: Yale University Press, 1990), p. 73.

is to define for subordinate groups what is realistic and what is not realistic and to drive certain aspirations and grievances into the realm of the impossible, of idle dreams. By persuading under-classes that their position, their life-chances, their tribulations are unalterable and inevitable, such a limited hegemony can produce the behavioral results of consent without necessarily changing peo-ple's values. Convinced that nothing can possibly be done to improve their situation and that it will always remain so, it is even conceivable that idle criticisms and hopeless aspirations would be eventually extinguished.[13]

But because 'the logic of domination represents a combination of historical and contemporary ideological and material practices that are never completely successful, always embody contradic-tions, and are constantly being fought over within asymmetrical relations of power',[14] organic intellectuals, who are able to learn from the poor and marginalized while simultaneously helping them to foster modes of self-education and struggle against vari-ous forms of oppression, are able to point to the spaces, contra-dictions and forms of resistance that raise the possibility for social struggle. However, and this is a key element of this analysis, oppressed people's accommodation to the logic of domination may mean that they actively resist emancipatory forms of knowl-edge offered by organic intellectuals.[15]

Such accounts of ideological hegemony argue that 'when op-pressed people live in silence, they use the words of their oppres-sors to describe their experience of oppression'. It is only within the praxis of liberation and in dialogue with organic intellectuals that it is possible for the poor and marginalized 'to break this silence and create their own language'.[16] So within liberation theologies, whether they be Latin American, black, womanist or feminist, the role of the intellectual is crucial in breaking 'the culture of silence'—in enabling a language and a speaking.

Working with a thin-ish theory of hegemony, Jean and John Comaroff nuance the kind of accounts discussed above by emph-

13. Scott, *Domination*, p. 74.

14. H.A. Giroux, 'Introduction', in Paulo Freire, *The Politics of Education* (London: Macmillan, 1985), pp. xi-xxv (xii).

15. Giroux, 'Introduction', pp. xviii-xxiii.

16. Frostin, *Liberation Theology in Tanzania*, p. 10.

asizing the instability and vulnerability of hegemony.[17] Drawing substantially on Antonio Gramsci, the Comaroffs pose a triangular relationship between culture, ideology and hegemony. Culture, they suggest, can be viewed as the shared repertoire of practices, symbols and meanings in which and with which the dialectics of domination and resistance operate. Hegemony and ideology are the two dominant forms in which power is entailed in culture. Placing power at the centre of their analysis of hegemony and ideology, the Comaroffs characterize hegemony and ideology as the two faces of power.

Hegemony is the nonagentive face of power that hides itself in the forms of everyday life; it is a form of power that is not always overtly felt in that 'it may not be experienced as power at all, since its effects are rarely wrought by overt compulsion'.

> They are internalized, in their negative guise, as constraints; in their neutral guise, as conventions; and, in their positive guise, as values. Yet the silent power of the sign, the unspoken authority of habit, may be as effective as the most violent coercion in shaping, directing, even dominating social thought and action.[18]

'Hegemony is that order of signs and practices, relations and distinctions, images and epistemologies—drawn from a historically situated cultural field—that come to be taken-for-granted as the natural and received shape of the world and everything that inhabits it'; its power lies in what it silences—what it prevents people from thinking and saying.[19]

Ideology is the agentive face of power that refers to the (relative) capacity of human beings to command and exercise control over the production, circulation and consumption of signs and objects in specific historical contexts. Ideology articulates and owns systems of meanings, values and beliefs for any group with a communal identity, whether dominant or subordinate, within a historically situated cultural field. While hegemony homogenizes, ideology articulates.[20]

17. Jean Comaroff and John Comaroff, *Of Revelation and Revolution: Christianity, Colonialism, and Consciousness in South Africa* (Chicago: University of Chicago Press, 1991), pp. 19-32.
18. Comaroff and Comaroff, *Of Revelation and Revolution*, p. 22.
19. Comaroff and Comaroff, *Of Revelation and Revolution*, p. 22.
20. Comaroff and Comaroff, *Of Revelation and Revolution*, p. 22.

The particularly creative and insightful contribution of the Comaroffs to this discussion is their suggestion that hegemony exists in reciprocal interdependence with ideology in that 'it is that part of a dominant worldview which has been naturalized'.[21] According to this account, hegemony and ideology are related along a continuum, with the hegemonic proportion of any dominant ideology being greater or lesser depending on the context and the control of the dominant. Typically, the making of hegemony requires the exercise of control over various modes of symbolic production, including educational and ritual processes, patterns of socialization, political and legal procedures, canons of style and self-representation, public policy and communication, health and bodily discipline, and so on. Hegemony is made when control is so sustained that it becomes deeply inscribed in the signs and practices of everyday life, becoming, to all intents and purposes, invisible. However, because the ideology of the dominant never occupies non-ideological terrain, while it might establish itself at the expense of prior ideologies, it seldom succeeds in totally subjecting what was there before. Hegemony 'is always threatened by the vitality that remains in the forms of life it thwarts'.[22] Consequently, along the hegemony/ideology continuum, the hegemonic is constantly being made—and, by the same token, may be unmade. Hegemony, then, 'is always intrinsically unstable, always vulnerable'.[23]

There remains a final element in the Comaroffs' construction. What differentiates one face of power from the other—hegemony from ideology—is the factor of human consciousness and the modes of representation that bear it. Rejecting 'the unspecified Cartesian assumptions about personhood, cognition, and social being that persist in mainstream Western thought, both orthodox and critical',[24] the Comaroffs suggest that it is much more plausible to see social knowledge and experience as situated along a chain of consciousness that is akin to the hegemony/ideology continuum. Consciousness, therefore, is a continuum 'whose two extremes are the unseen and the seen, the submerged and the

21. Comaroff and Comaroff, *Of Revelation and Revolution*, p. 25.
22. Comaroff and Comaroff, *Of Revelation and Revolution*, p. 25.
23. Comaroff and Comaroff, *Of Revelation and Revolution*, p. 27.
24. Comaroff and Comaroff, *Of Revelation and Revolution*, p. 28.

apprehended, the unrecognized and the cognized'.[25] And so just as hegemonies and ideologies shift in relation to one another, so too consciousness may shift between these poles.

> One the one hand, the submerged, the unseen, the unrecognized may under certain conditions be called to awareness; on the other, things once perceived and explicitly marked may slip below the level of discourse into the unremarked recesses of the collective unconscious [that] is the implicit structure of shared meaning that human beings absorb as they learn to be members of a particular social world.[26]

Along the continuum between the conscious and the unconscious, the Comaroffs argue, 'lies the most critical domain of all' for the analysis of domination and resistance.

> It is the realm of partial recognition, of inchoate awareness, of ambiguous perception, and, sometimes, of creative tension; that liminal space of human experience in which people discern acts and facts but cannot or do not order them into narrative descriptions or even into articulate conceptions of the world; in which signs and events are observed, but in a hazy, translucent light; in which individuals or groups know that something is happening to them but find it difficult to put their fingers on quite what it is. It is from this realm…that silent signifiers and unmarked practices may rise to the level of consciousness, of ideological assertion, and become the subject of overt political and social contestation—or from which they may recede into the hegemonic, to languish there unremarked for the time being.[27]

This is also the realm from which the poets and organic intellectuals draw the innovative impulses that give voice to the struggles of the people.[28]

But what if this analysis is inadequate and the poor and marginalized have not accommodated themselves to the logic of domination? What if they already have a language and already speak? What if the hegemonic/ideological continuum is *always* contested? What if the hegemonic is constantly having to be made *because* it is always being unmade? What if we take out the 'but

25. Comaroff and Comaroff, *Of Revelation and Revolution*, p. 29.
26. Comaroff and Comaroff, *Of Revelation and Revolution*, p. 29.
27. Comaroff and Comaroff, *Of Revelation and Revolution*, p. 29.
28. Comaroff and Comaroff, *Of Revelation and Revolution*, p. 29.

cannot' in the quote immediately above this paragraph? Without denying the richness of the Comaroffs' contribution, which I will continue to draw from, such moves as my questions contemplate would seriously undermine even a thin version of hegemony. These are questions that reflection on the contextual Bible study process in South Africa has begun to generate. James Scott's work on 'domination and the arts of resistance' has been particularly useful in helping us to reflect more deeply and carefully on our experience and practice.

Scott problematizes both thick and thin versions of ideological hegemony, and so too the relationship between the socially engaged biblical scholar and ordinary 'readers' of the Bible in poor and marginalized communities. In his detailed study of domination and resistance we find a more nuanced analysis, which argues that theories of hegemony and false consciousness do not take account of what he calls 'the hidden transcript'. 'The hidden transcript' is the discourse, including speech acts and a whole range of other practices,[29] that subordinate groups create in response to their ordeal of domination—a discourse 'that represents a critique of power spoken behind the back of the dominant'.[30] Behind the scenes, subordinate groups 'create and defend a social space in which offstage dissent to the official transcript of power relations may be voiced'.[31] The practices and rituals of denigration and domination routinely generated by slavery, serfdom, the caste system, colonialism, patriarchy and racism usually deny subordinates the ordinary response of asserting their dignity through negative reciprocity: a slap for a slap, an insult for an insult.[32] Instead, subordinates establish their dignity, register their resistance, and elaborate their hidden transcript a restricted 'public' or social circle that excludes—that is hidden from—certain specified others.[33] In this relatively safe space subordinates find a par-

29. Among these other practices are activities such as poaching, pilfering, clandestine tax evasion, intentionally shabby work, and so on; Scott, *Domination*, pp. 14, 118, 189-94.

30. Scott, *Domination*, p. xii.

31. Scott, *Domination*, p. xi.

32. Scott, *Domination*, pp. xi-xii.

33. In instances those excluded may include members of a subordinate community that have voluntarily embraced the dominant ideology in order to occupy positions of power (see Scott, *Domination*, p. 82) or sectors of the

tial refuge from the humiliations of domination. Suffering from the same humiliations and subject to the same terms of domination, subordinates for whom survival is the primary objective 'have a shared interest in jointly creating a discourse of dignity, of negation, and of justice. They have, in addition, a shared interest in concealing a social site apart from domination where such a hidden transcript can be elaborated in comparative safety.'[34]

The hidden transcript represents the safe articulation and acting out of forms of resistance and defiance that is usually thwarted in contexts where the exercise of power is nearly constant. 'Discretion in the face of power requires that a part of the "self" that would reply or strike back must lie low. It is this self that finds expression in the safer realm of the hidden transcript'.[35] The hidden transcript speaks what must normally be choked back and takes back the speech or behaviour that seemed unavoidable and was required for survival in power-laden encounters with the dominant.[36]

The crucial point of Scott's detailed argument is that 'the hidden transcript is a self-disclosure that power relations normally exclude from the official transcript'.[37] The public transcript—the open interaction between subordinates and those who dominate—where it is not positively misleading, is unlikely to tell the whole story about power relations, because it is frequently in the interest of both parties to conspire tacitly in misrepresentation.[38]

It would be a mistake, Scott argues, to see the discourse of deference and subordination merely as performances extracted by power; such discourse also serves as a barrier and a veil that the dominant find difficult or impossible to penetrate. The appearances that power requires are, to be sure, forcefully imposed, but this does not preclude 'their active use as a means of resistance

---

community that dominate other sectors, for example men over women or the not-yet-disabled over the disabled. In other words, there are for any particular actor several public and hidden transcripts, depending on the context and the audience addressed (Scott, *Domination*, p. 14 n. 24).

34. Scott, *Domination*, pp. 113-15.
35. Scott, *Domination*, p. 114.
36. Scott, *Domination*, pp. 18, 114-15.
37. Scott, *Domination*, pp. 113-15.
38. Scott, *Domination*, p. 2.

and evasion'.[39] While evasion comes at the considerable cost of contributing to the production of a public transcript that *apparently* ratifies the social ideology of the dominant, where the script for survival is rigid and the consequences of a mistake severe, the appearance of conformity is a necessary tactic.[40] Within the normal constraints of domination subordinates have both 'a vested interest in avoiding any *explicit* display of subordination' and 'a practical interest in resistance'. 'The reconciliation of these two objectives that seem at cross-purposes is typically achieved by pursuing precisely those forms of resistance that avoid any open confrontation with the structures of authority being resisted.' 'The greater the power exerted over them and the closer the survelliance, the more incentive subordinates have to foster the impression of compliance, agreement, deference.'[41] The goal of subordinate groups, as they conduct their ideological and material resistance, is precisely to escape detection, and the extent that they achieve their goal, such activities do not appear in the archives. 'In this respect, subordinate groups are complicitous in contributing to a sanitized official transcript, for that is one way they cover their tracks.'[42]

The dominant, for their part, also play a role in maintaining the appearance of a public transcript of deference and compliance. To call attention to detected forms of resistance and defiance might expose the fissures in their power and erode their authority and perhaps encourage other acts of insubordination. Elites, in other words, 'have their own compelling reasons to preserve a public facade of unity, willing compliance, and respect'[43] and so to keep conflict out of the public record.

So 'unless one can penetrate the official transcript of both subordinates and elites, a reading of the social evidence will almost always represent a confirmation of the status quo in hegemonic terms'.[44] The strategic appearances that elites and subordinates alike ordinarily insert into the public transcript make it a very

39. Scott, *Domination*, p. 32.
40. Scott, *Domination*, pp. 32-33.
41. Scott, *Domination*, pp. 89-90.
42. Scott, *Domination*, pp. 86-90.
43. Scott, *Domination*, p. 90.
44. Scott, *Domination*, p. 90.

unreliable vehicle for social analysis. 'The official transcript of power relations *is* a sphere in which power appears naturalized because that is what elites exert their influence to produce and because it ordinarily serves the immediate interests of subordinates to avoid discrediting these appearances.'[45] You cannot believe all you read in the public transcript! A comparison of the hidden transcript of the weak with that of the powerful, who also develop a hidden transcript representing the practices and claims of their rule that cannot be openly avowed, and of *both* hidden transcripts to the public transcript of power relations offers a substantially new way of understanding resistance to domination.[46]

But is there still not a case for Gramsci's notion of the dominated consciousness of subordinate groups? For Gramsci hegemony works primarily at the level of thought as distinct from the level of action.[47] Scott turns this around. He considers 'subordinate classes *less* constrained at the level of thought and ideology, since they can in secluded settings speak with comparative safety, and *more* constrained at the level of political action and struggle, where the daily exercise of power sharply limits the options available to them'.[48] So, Scott argues, subordinate groups have typically learned, in situations short of those rare all-or-nothing struggles, 'to clothe their resistance and defiance in ritualisms of subordination that serve both to disguise their purposes and to provide them with a ready route of retreat that may soften the consequences of a possible failure'.[49] This is because most protests and challenges—even quite violent ones—'are made in the realistic expectation that the central features of the form of domination will remain intact'.[50] Consequently, '[m]ost acts of power from below, even when they are protests—implicitly or explicitly—will largely observe the "rules" even if their objective is to undermine them'.[51]

45. Scott, *Domination*, pp. 87-90.

46. Scott, *Domination*, p. xii.

47. Antonio Gramsci, *Selections from the Prison Notebooks* (ed. and trans. Quintin Hoare and Geoffrey Nowel Smith; London: Lawrence and Wishart, 1971), p. 333.

48. Scott, *Domination*, p. 91.

49. Scott, *Domination*, p. 96.

50. Scott, *Domination*, p. 93.

51. Scott, *Domination*, p. 93.

Scott believes that 'the historical evidence clearly shows that subordinate groups have been capable of revolutionary *thought* that repudiates existing forms of domination'.[52] However, because the occasions on which subordinate groups have been able to act openly and fully on that thought are rare, the conflict will usually take 'a dialogic form in which the language of the dialogue will invariably borrow heavily from the terms of the dominant ideology prevailing in the public transcript'.[53] The dominant discourse becomes, then, 'a plastic idiom or dialect that is capable of carrying an enormous variety of meanings, including those that are subversive of their use as intended by the dominant', for in most contexts of domination 'the terrain of dominant discourse is the only plausible arena of struggle'.[54] So by recognizing that adopting and adapting the dominant discourse is a guise induced by power relations that is necessary outside of the safety of the hidden transcript, and by learning to read the dialects and codes generated by the techniques and arts of resistance, we can discern a dialogue with power in the public transcript.[55]

So instead of focusing on the public transcript, which represents the formal relations between the powerful and weak, as most social analysis does, we should attempt to 'read, interpret, and understand the often fugitive political conduct of subordinate groups'.[56] A focus on 'a partly sanitized, ambiguous, and coded version of the hidden transcript' that is always present in the public discourse of subordinate groups in the form of rumours, gossip, folktales, songs, gestures, jokes, theatre and other forms of popular culture, reveals forms of resistance, defiance and critical consciousness.[57] In the words of the Ethiopian proverb with which Scott opens his study, 'When the great lord passes the wise peasant bows deeply and silently farts'. Theories of ideological hegemony look at the stage, the public transcript of the bowing

52. Scott, *Domination*, p. 101.

53. Scott, *Domination*, p. 102.

54. Scott, *Domination*, pp. 102-103.

55. Scott, *Domination*, pp. 101-103, 138.

56. Scott, *Domination*, p. xii. See Jean Comaroff, *Body of Power, Spirit of Resistance: The Culture and History of a South African People* (Chicago: University of Chicago Press, 1985), p. 261 for a similar point. See also Cochrane, 'Circles of Dignity', p. 107.

57. Scott, *Domination*, p. 19.

peasant. Scott draws our attention to what is hidden, offstage, the silent fart.

Any analysis of the relationship between the socially engaged biblical scholar and the ordinary poor and marginalized 'reader' of the Bible is incomplete that does not take into account a more nuanced understanding of domination and resistance. While the role of the intellectual, whether organic or other, seems fairly clear in analyses of domination and resistance that hold to strong notions of hegemony, the role of the intellectual is less clear given Scott's analysis. In this analysis subordinate groups are already engaged in forms of resistance and already have a language. The culture of silence is a strategy and not the whole story. What is hidden is hidden for good reason, so any attempt to penetrate the disguise is dangerous. And when dignity and autonomy demand an irruption or an articulation, this must be done in ways determined by the dominated. There does not appear to be a silence to break or a language to create.

Yet ordinary 'readers' of the Bible in poor and marginalized communities do call socially engaged biblical scholars to read the Bible with them. Why they do so is not clear given the discussion of the previous pages, but it must, it seems reasonable to assume, have something to do with our biblical training. I will probe the possible contributions our training might make in the following chapters. But while the 'why' may not be clear, the parameters of 'how' we participate are. Our discussion thus far makes it clear why both a naive 'listening to', that romanticizes and idealizes the interpretations of the poor and marginalized, and a patronizing 'speaking for', that minimizes and rationalizes the interpretations of the poor and marginalized, must be problematized.

'Listening to' presupposes that we are listening to the 'real' voice—the hidden transcript—of a subject, and fails to take sufficient account of contestation taking place in the community between the public and the hidden transcript, particularly when we are present—particularly when 'we' are people like me who are not *organic* intellectuals. The frontier between the public and the hidden transcript is a zone of constant contestation, the boundaries of which are continually a site of struggle. Furthermore, given that the hidden transcript is specific to a given social site and to a particular set of subjects, and that for any subject there are always several public and hidden transcripts, depending on the audience being addressed, the 'authentic' voice of the sub-altern subject is difficult to determine. This does not entail, how-ever, that they have no identity and no voice. While I applaud the postmodernist deconstruction of the grand narratives of Western history (and philosophy and theology and biblical studies) with their foundationalism of subject-centred reason,[58] I resist the view 'that autonomy is, in any practical sense, impossible since one is always already radically situated in a linguistic culture'.[59] The postmodern angst of middle-class intellectuals and its accom-panying analysis is inadequate. '[T]he *jouissance* which issues from postmodernism's decentring of the subject is unlikely to be shared by those who, for reasons of gender, class, race, and sexuality, have never experienced or possessed (even as an illusion) a coher-ent subjectivity.'[60] 'To recognize the limitations of an ideal which was never one's own is to bear a very different relationship to its perceived loss.'[61] While we can cautiously accept postmodern challenges to the coherent, autonomous subject we must 'work first to assert and affirm a denied or alienated subjectivity'.[62] This does not require, however, 'the resurrection of the subject of humanism', since, for example, both feminism and post-colonial-ism cannot naively ignore the force of postmodernism's critique of Enlightenment epistemology as rooted in the instrumental domination of inert object (body, world, nature, woman, colo-nized), by a detached and transcendent subject (mind, self, sci-ence, man, colonizer).[63] In the absence of grand narratives we may still find opportunities to construct 'shifting and provisional

58. Jean-François Lyotard, *The Postmodern Condition: A Report on Knowledge* (Minneapolis: University of Minnesota Press, 1984).

59. Michael Marais, 'Reading Postmodernism(s): A Review Essay', *Current Writing* 5 (1993), pp. 134-41 (136); Patricia Waugh, *Practising Postmodernism/ Reading Modernism* (London: Edward Arnold, 1992).

60. Marais, 'Reading Postmodernism(s)', p. 137.

61. Waugh, *Practising Postmodernism*, p. 125.

62. Linda Hutcheon, 'Circling the Downspout of Empire', in Ian Adam and Helen Tiffin (eds.), *Past the Last Post: Theorizing Post-colonialism and Post-modernism* (New York: Harvester, 1991), pp. 167-89 (168); Marais, 'Reading Postmodernism(s)', p. 137.

63. Marais, 'Reading Postmodernism(s)', p. 137, citing Waugh, *Practising Postmodernism*, p. 120.

identities for ourselves in the competing language games which proliferate in the various contexts which make up our lives'.[64] Instead of adopting a postmodern perspective which nihilistically dissolves self, we can construct postmodernism as a form of discourse which attempts to 'renegotiate modes of relationship'. Using arguments similar to those of Jurgen Habermas, and drawing on resources from feminist discourse, Patricia Waugh 'demonstrates that it is possible to arrive at such a model, which stresses relationship and connection rather than separation and objectivity as the markers of identity'.[65] Making particular reference to the relevance of Waugh's work for South Africa, Michael Marais argues that Waugh's work 'points to the existence…of a project aimed at negotiating alternative models of subjectivity to both Descartes' rational "I" and the anarchic dispersal of *jouissance* suggested by anti-humanist discourse'.[66]

So, in the words of Spivak, instead of 'invocations of the *authenticity* of the Other'—attempting an essentialist search for lost origins—accenting 'the mechanics of the constitution of the Other' would be more analytic and useful.[67] In other words, we must move beyond 'listening to' and take account of the forces and factors that constitute the fractured subjectivity of the other,[68] as for example Mary McClintock Fulkerson does in her careful case studies of the analytics of women's discourse within the constraints of particular communities of women in particular contexts.[69]

Furthermore, 'listening to' does not sufficiently emphasize the dimensions of discourse that constitute the hidden transcript. Scott and the Comaroffs agree that the range of forms of discourse is great, including speech acts, gestures, performances, rituals, and many other practices, and that the dimensions of

64. Marais, 'Reading Postmodernism(s)', p. 137; Lyotard, *The Postmodern Condition*, pp. 14-18.

65. Marais, 'Reading Postmodernism(s)', p. 138; Waugh, *Practising Postmodernism*, p. 125.

66. Marais, 'Reading Postmodernism(s)', p. 140.

67. Gayatri C. Spivak, 'Can the Subaltern Speak?', in Gary Nelson and L. Grossberg (eds.), *Marxism and the Interpretation of Culture* (London: Macmillan, 1988), pp. 271-313 (291-95).

68. Spivak, 'Can the Subaltern Speak?', p. 278.

69. Mary McClintock Fulkerson, *Changing the Subject: Women's Discourses and Feminist Theology* (Minneapolis: Fortress Press, 1994).

discourse extend from the incipient and inchoate to the explicit and articulate. The subaltern does speak, but in forms of discourse that we cannot hear if we only listen.

Even more problematic is 'speaking for'. 'Speaking for' quite simply dismisses or minimizes the hidden transcript—the speaking voice of the subaltern—and denies the subject status of the poor and oppressed altogether. The seduction for intellectuals, including socially engaged biblical scholars, and the fear for those they work with, is that the positionality of the intellectual is elided.[70] The dangerousness of the intellectual lies in his or her 'masquerading as the absent nonrepresenter who lets the oppressed speak for themselves'.[71] In 'speaking for', or speaking on-behalf-of, the role of the intellectual in selectively constructing the subjectivity of the other, in re-presenting them, is hidden. In the relay race of representing the other the intellectual becomes transparent.[72] There should be no *interpretation* without representation—no interpretation from above.[73] Socially engaged biblical scholars must move beyond 'speaking for' and mark their positionality as participating subjects.

We can only move beyond 'speaking for' and 'listening to' if we are willing to enter into a 'speaking with'.[74] I use the phrase 'speaking/reading with', following Jill Arnott's reading of Gayatri Spivak, to point to 'the need to occupy the dialectical space between two subject-positions, without ever allowing either to become transparent'.[75] This requires that we socially engaged biblical scholars remain constantly alert to, and interrogative of, our own positionality and that of our discourse partners, so as to ensure that the mediating process of representation remains

70. Spivak, 'Can the Subaltern Speak?', p. 294.

71. Spivak, 'Can the Subaltern Speak?', p. 292.

72. Spivak, 'Can the Subaltern Speak?', p. 279.

73. Osayande Obery Hendricks, 'Guerilla Exegesis: "Struggle" as a Scholarly Vocation: A Postmodern Approach to African-American Interpretation', *Semeia* 72 (1995), pp. 73-90 (82).

74. Spivak uses the phrase 'speaking to', but I prefer the preposition 'with'.

75. Jill Arnott, 'French Feminism in a South African Frame? Gayatri Spivak and the Problem of "Representation" in South African Feminism', in M.J. Daymond (ed.), *South African Feminisms: Writing, Theory, and Criticism, 1990–1994* (New York and London: Garland, 1996), pp. 77-89 (85).

visible. In other words, with Arnott and Spivak, I am arguing that 'speaking/reading with' takes seriously the subjectivity of both the biblical scholar and the ordinary poor and marginalized 'reader' of the Bible, and all that this entails for their respective resources, categories and contributions.

'Reading with' is clearly contested terrain, the contours of which are difficult to chart. But we can learn much from cultural feminism's and postmodernist feminism's critique of the notion of universal experience and subjectivity. Underlying their critique is the postmodern understanding that individual and communal selves are always in the process of being constructed and negotiated,[76] and that we must therefore consider more carefully and exactly, in the words of Kathleen Weiler, those forces 'in which individuals shape themselves and by which they are shaped'.[77] This understanding of subjectivity as 'the constant creation and negotiation of selves within structures of ideology and material constraints' challenges, for example, 'the use of such universal terms as oppression and liberation without locating these claims in a concrete historical or social context'.[78] Clearly, recognizing that subjects are shaped by their particular experience of class, race, gender, culture and other social forces has powerful implications for the process of 'reading with', in that it emphasizes the need to make conscious the subject positions of both socially engaged biblical scholars and ordinary 'readers' of the Bible.

However, the challenge not only consists of the need 'to articulate and claim a particular historical and social identity, to locate ourselves', but also of the need 'to build coalitions from a recognition of the partial knowledges of our own constructed iden-

76. See, for example, Kathleen M. Kirby, 'Thinking through the Boundary: The Politics of Location, Subjects, and Space', *Boundary 2* 20 (1993), pp. 173-89; and Mary Ann Tolbert, 'Reading for Liberation', in Fernando F. Segovia and Mary Ann Tolbert (eds.), *Reading from This Place: Social Location and Biblical Interpretation in the United States* (Minneapolis: Fortress Press, 1995), pp. 263-73 (265-66).

77. Kathleen Weiler, 'Freire and a Feminist Pedagogy of Difference', *Harvard Educational Review* 61 (1991), pp. 449-74 (467).

78. Weiler, 'Feminist Pedagogy', p. 469.

tities'.[79] So while particularity and partiality are a constant reminder that the process of 'reading with' is contested, they also
offer us, in our process of becoming, creative ways of being partially constituted by each other's subjectivities.

While we must recognize that our claims are contingent and situated and while we must acknowledge that our own histories and
selves are in process, Weiler stresses that recognizing and acknowledging the presence of difference 'does not mean abandonment
of the goals of social justice and empowerment'.[80] Foregrounding
our subjectivities and positionalities enables us to attempt to build
coalitions around common goals rather than a denial of
difference. Elizabeth Ellsworth makes a similar point when she
argues that

> Realizing that there are partial narratives that some social groups
> or cultures have and others can never know, but that are necessary
> for survival, is a condition to embrace and use as an opportunity to
> build a kind of social and educational interdependency that rec-
> ognizes differences as 'different strengths' and as 'forces for
> change'.[81]

And in the words of Audre Lorde, 'Difference must be not
merely tolerated, but seen as a fund of necessary polarities between which our creativity can spark like a dialectic. Only then
does the necessity for interdependency become unthreatening.'[82]

It must be continually stressed, however, that the power relations in the interface between the ordinary reader and the biblical
scholar cannot be obliterated, and they must not be ignored. They
must be foregrounded. Postmodern feminists like Arnott, Spivak,
Ellsworth and Lorde emphasize the creative and constructive
potential of 'a genuinely dialectical interaction between two vigilantly foregrounded subject-positions'.[83] Only then can we move

79. Weiler, 'Feminist Pedagogy', p. 470.

80. Weiler, 'Feminist Pedagogy', p. 470.

81. Elizabeth Ellsworth, 'Why Doesn't This Feel Empowering? Working
through the Repressive Myths of Critical Pedagogy', *Harvard Educational
Review* 59 (1989), pp. 297-324 (319).

82. Audre Lorde, *Sister Outsider* (New York: The Crossing Press, 1984),
p. 112; see also Ellsworth, 'Why Doesn't This Feel Empowering?', p. 319.

83. Arnott, 'French Feminism', p. 87.

beyond 'speaking for' and 'listening to' towards a place where difference enables.

Such talk of an interdependency between biblical scholars and ordinary readers of the Bible from poor and marginalized communities can be threatening and unsettling in the corridors of the academy, and it certainly involves risk. But in the suffering and pain of KwaZulu-Natal we have come to recognize the necessity of interdependency and a need for 'an ethic of risk' which requires that we recognize the partiality of our particular choices *and* that we continue to struggle for full liberation and life.[84] For us, reading the Bible and doing theology in this interface calls for dialogue and difference: a 'speaking with' which vigilantly foregrounds both the readings and resources of socially engaged biblical scholars and the readings and resources of the poor and marginalized.[85]

Usually the connection between our work as biblical scholars and our life commitments is covert, and if our work is to be used by others we want to remain in control. But clearly the interface I have outlined above, and to which I will return below, demands an overt connection between our biblical research and our social commitments, and that we risk allowing our work and ourselves to be used by others without our control. This requires something of a conversion 'from below'. Biblical scholars must be born 'from below'. My use of the term 'conversion' is not simply for dramaturgical effect; to be of use to others is not easy, it is difficult. Offering ourselves and our resources may be costly, choosing collaboration instead of conversation may be painful, and participating in a reading process that is often eclectic and strategic may be disturbing. So we do need to be converted.

Although our conversion is more a function of our contextual commitments than our scholarship, implicit in my discussion so far are at least five threads, within biblical studies, that facilitate such a conversion. My point here, and I will not labour it, is that

84. Welch, *Communities of Resistance*, p. 26.

85. Gerald O. West, 'Difference and Dialogue: Reading the Joseph Story *with* Poor and Marginalized Communities in South Africa', *Biblical Interpretation* 2 (1994), pp. 152-70.

we have resources which are already to some extent a part of our practice which may be of help if we are prepared to change. The presence of liberation hermeneutics within biblical studies, albeit from the margins of the discipline, is the most obvious. As I have already charted the contribution of liberation hermeneutics, I will only reiterate the basic insight of liberation theologies and their methodological starting point, 'that all theology knowingly or not is by definition always engaged for or against the oppressed'.[86] Liberation hermeneutics asks, somewhat stridently, biblical scholars to make an option for the poor and marginalized, and to accept the consequences of this choic for our reading practice.

Living in the shadow of liberation hermeneutics, and, many would argue, constituting a part of liberation hermeneutics, is a second guide towards conversion: inculturation hermeneutics or cultural exegesis. Culture has often had a secondary place in contexts where liberation hermeneutics have held the primary position. Whereas race, class and gender have been the focal concerns of liberation hermeneutics, culture is the focus of inculturation hermeneutics. Our disease with the metanarratives that have declared popular religion to be 'the opiate of the people' (Marx) and the more nuanced understanding of resistance to domination discussed above require that we begin with the categories and concepts of local communities of the poor and marginalized— categories and concepts which are shaped by the cultural as well as the socio-political. Post-colonial Africa, Latin America, post-apartheid South Africa and the edges of the First World, for example, are uncovering and recovering culture, although it is not yet clear what forms these recoveries will take.[87] But what is

---

86. Elisabeth Schüssler Fiorenza, *Bread Not Stone: The Challenge of Feminist Biblical Interpretation* (Boston: Beacon Press, 1984), p. 45.

87. Sugirtharajah, *Voices from the Margin*; Segovia and Tolbert (eds.), *Reading from This Place*; Daniel Smith-Christopher (ed.), *Text and Experience: Towards a Cultural Exegesis of the Bible* (The Biblical Seminar, 35; Sheffield: Sheffield Academic Press, 1995); Hannah W. Kinoti and John M. Waliggo (eds.), *The Bible in African Christianity: Essays in Biblical Theology* (Nairobi: Acton Publishers, 1997); Justin Ukpong, 'Rereading the Bible with African Eyes', *Journal of Theology for Southern Africa* 91 (1995), pp. 3-14; Benjamin A. Ntreh, 'Towards an African Biblical Hermeneutic', *Africa Theological Journal* 19 (1990), pp. 247-54; Cheryl J. Saunders (ed.), *Living the Intersection: Womanism and Afrocentrism in Theology* (Minneapolis: Fortress Press, 1995).

clear is that the Bible is itself a cultural product, that it came to Africa, as elsewhere, as part of colonizing and conquering cultures, and that ordinary 'readers' have always brought their cultural resources to their readings of the Bible. So as biblical scholarship becomes increasingly aware of the forms of cultural complicity in its reading practices, it can choose to embrace the cultural constructs of others.

A third, more polite, conversion-enabling thread can be found in the various postmodernisms and poststructuralisms within biblical studies. As Cornel West argues at length, postmodern points of view can serve as a useful springboard for a more engaged, even subversive, philosophical perspective. This is so primarily because they encourage the cultivation of critical attitudes towards all philosophical traditions, inducing a crucial shift in the subject matter of philosophers 'from the grounding of beliefs to the scrutiny of groundless traditions—from epistemology to ethics, truth to practices, foundations to consequences' and, in so doing, such postmodern perspectives have the potential to lend themselves to emancipatory ends in that they propose 'the tenuous self-images and provisional vocabularies that undergird past and present social orders as central objects of criticism'.[88] And, as Cornel West continues, such shifts are particularly significant for those on the underside of history because 'oppressed people have more at stake than others in focusing on the tenuous and provisional vocabularies which have had and do have hegemonic status in past and present societies'.[89] There is no 'given' out there or in here that cannot be unmade, deconstructed, and refigured along local lines. Without minimizing the terrifying forms of control still concentrated at the centre, the cracks that keep appearing in the totalizing discourse of the dominant make ways for local articulations and languages which were only previously present as traces.

88. Cornel West, 'Afterword: The Politics of American Neo-Pragmatism', in J. Rajchman and C. West (eds.), *Post-Analytic Philosophy* (New York: Columbia University Press, 1985), p. 270.
89. West, 'Afterword', pp. 270-71.

Moreover, postmodern impulses and moments, in dialogue with other more engaged forms of discourse that dare to dream,[90] provide possibilities for real alliances between socially engaged biblical scholars who, on the one side, are transacting with the interface between modernity and postmodernity and ordinary African (Third World) readers of the Bible who, on the other side, are transacting with the interface between the pre-modern and the modern.[91] While modernity cannot be completely un-made, its claim to mastery [*sic*] and control can be challenged by those who transact with it on either side. The postmodern shift, more specifically, allows biblical scholars to abandon their quest for the certainty of 'the right' reading in favour of the more human concern for useful readings and resources—readings and resources that are a part of a discourse that takes seriously questions of ethics, practices, and effects. Postmodernism, with its destabilizing of the interpretative process and its decentring of the interpretations of experts, gives opportunity to the different subjectivities of others, including the poor and marginalized—the most 'other'. Our 'incredulity toward metanarratives'[92] and the indeterminacy of deconstruction provide a place for the particularity and partiality of the readings of others.

Intimately intertwined with the above three threads is a fourth thread, that of post-colonial criticism. Post-colonial criticism is

90. See Gerald West, *Biblical Hermeneutics of Liberation: Modes of Reading the Bible in the South African Context* (Pietermaritzburg: Cluster Publications, 2nd rev. edn, 1995), pp. 35-36, 39-41 where I discuss Cornel West's claim that postmodernism does not know how to dream—to reconstruct after deconstructing.

91. The term 'pre-modern' is not used here in a pejorative sense. However, we should note that the very possibility of the term having a pejorative connotation 'is reflective of the hegemony of the modern project and its own ability to stigmatize all that does not become swept up into its influence' (Anthony O. Balcomb, 'Modernity and the African Experience', *Bulletin for Contextual Theology in Southern Africa and Africa* 3 [1996], pp. 12-20). In this article Tony Balcomb analyses the transactions at the interface between the modern and the pre-modern. See also Jean Comaroff and John Comaroff, *Modernity and its Malcontents: Ritual and Power in Postcolonial Africa* (Chicago: University of Chicago Press, 1993).

92. Lyotard, *The Postmodern Condition*, p. xxiv.

something of a cottage industry in literary studies, particularly in Euro-American contexts but increasingly in South Africa as well. Post-colonial concerns are also on the way to becoming another 'criticism' within biblical studies, alongside the other more familiar criticisms. However, the geographical (and political) pattern here is rather different, with post-colonial biblical criticism being located primarily in Southern/Third World contexts or among their diasporial exiles and emigres who live in the North. But, no doubt, post-colonial discourse within biblical studies will make the shift from East to West and from South to North, as it has done in literary studies, altering its forms as it moves from projects which struggle to change the world to programmes which re-describe the world.[93]

My use of post-colonial criticism, already evident in my discussion, includes two key elements: *resistance* to *colonial representations*. Post-colonial criticism may be useful in that it offers resources for resisting (by de-constructing) surviving forms of subjectivity, self-apprehension and othering that have been constituted in a colonial past.[94] This use of 'post-colonial' recognizes that while post-colonial criticism 'relies on theories derived from 'postmodernism' (including poststructuralism) in order to argue for the historical contingency of colonial forms of knowledge and culture (as against the claim to "universality" in colonial forms of knowledge)',[95] it resists 'the totalised version of the determination of the subject that one occasionally finds in poststructuralism'.[96] So if post-colonialism is to have any usefulness it must, like feminism, for example, have a distinct political agenda that compels it 'to go beyond the postmodern limits of deconstructing existing orthodoxies into the realms of social and political action'.[97]

Post-colonial criticism, then, has the potential to bind the three previous threads together. For example, in a recent meeting between socially engaged biblical scholars from Nigeria and South

93. Jasper Goss, 'Postcolonialism: Subverting Whose Empire?', *Third World Quarterly* 17 (1996), pp. 239-50 (246).

94. Leon de Kock, 'Postcolonial Analysis and the Question of Critical Disablement', *Current Writing* 5 (1993), pp. 44-69 (65).

95. De Kock, 'Postcolonial Analysis', p. 44.

96. David Attwell, 'Introduction', *Current Writing* 5 (1993), pp. 1-6 (4).

97. Hutcheon, 'Circling the Downspout of Empire', p. 168.

Africa it was agreed that we needed to construct an interface between inculturation hermeneutics (the emphasis of the Nigerians) and liberation hermeneutics (the emphasis of the South Africans). This is one potential contribution of post-colonial hermeneutics: it holds together the concerns of liberation hermeneutics (race, class and gender) with the concerns of inculturation hermeneutics (culture). Also, the 'post' in post-colonial hermeneutics draws postmodern moves into our reading processes, and reminds us of the historical contingency of colonial forms/structures of knowledge and culture. But because the 'post' in post-colonial hermeneutics is not the same as the 'post' in 'postmodernism', we are able to resist not only the domination of colonial forms/structures of knowledge and culture, but also to resist the usual alternatives of the play of pluralism or the abyss of meaninglessness offered by postmodernism.[98] Post-colonial criticism has a distinct political agenda. Furthermore, in my construction of post-colonial criticism, post-colonial criticism foregrounds relationship and connection rather than separation and objectivity as the markers of identity. For the socially engaged biblical scholar difference must not be an end in itself—apartheid has already travelled that road; instead, difference is the constant reminder that we must choose to be partially constructed by collaboration with others, particularly those who are most 'other'.

The fifth thread is less obvious, but also offers a potential path for conversion. Reader-response criticism, or reception hermeneutics, has introduced biblical scholars to a reader who is no longer perceived as a passive receiver of authorial or textual meaning, but who is now recognized as an active creator of meaning.[99] While real ordinary readers of the Bible have never been fully admitted to the guild of 'proper' readers,[100] the logic of this

98. West, *Biblical Hermeneutics*, p. 152; David Jobling, 'Writing the Wrongs of the World: The Deconstruction of the Biblical Text in the Context of Liberation Theologies', *Semeia* 51 (1990), pp. 81-118.

99. See Bernard C. Lategan, 'Current Issues in the Hermeneutic Debate', *Neotestamentica* 18 (1984), pp. 1-17 (3-4).

100. Stephen D. Moore, *Literary Criticism and the Gospels Today: Landmarks, Fault Lines, Time Zones* (New Haven: Yale University Press, 1989).

approach demands their presence. The practice of 'reading with' invites scholarly readers, and their allied 'implied' readers and other surrogates,[101] to read the Bible with actual readers from poor and marginalized communities, even when many of these readers are only 'readers' in a metaphorical sense. Those from the margins who have been waiting in the wings, offstage, who are not usually invited to the comfortable coffee table (because, of course, they do not wear a collar and tie nor do they have the money for filter coffee!),[102] may be heard, if we have ears to hear, calling us to come read with them.

These threads, in their different ways, are reminders that every discourse, including our own as biblical scholars, 'bears within itself the anonymous and repressed actuality of highly particular arrangements of power and knowledge'.[103] Our discourse has excluded others, particularly those who might disrupt and challenge the established hierarchies of our academies and societies. But 'they' are not silent, and will not be silenced. These five threads that weave their way through our discipline are reminders of what we already know: that our voices are not the only ones. The voices, whether inchoate or articulate, from the edges of our globalized village—the voices of the victims of our discourses and our history—cannot be ignored if we are to become more human and more whole. What we hear may be strident and uncivil—in a word, other—and they are, but when we do hear we might discover, above our own chatter, possibilities we have never dared to dream.[104]

Inhabiting the weave of these threads calls for an ethic of risk which requires *both* that I recognize the partiality of my particular place and the choices I make *and* that I continue to struggle with particular communities of the poor and oppressed. A pluralism that masks 'a genial confusion in which one tries to enjoy the

101. See Timothy M.S. Long, 'A Real Reader Reading *Revelation*', *Semeia* 73 (1996), pp. 79-107.

102. Terry Eagleton, *The Function of Criticism: From the Spectator to Post-Structuralism* (London: Verso, 1984).

103. Tracy, *Plurality and Ambiguity*, p. 79. Tracy is here drawing on the work of Foucault.

104. Tracy, *Plurality and Ambiguity*, p. 79.

pleasures of difference without ever committing oneself to any particular vision of resistance and hope' is not enough.[105] Our reading practice must be located within a particular vision of resistance and hope which includes solidarity with the poor and marginalized. And, as the next four chapters will demonstrate, we do seem to have something to offer as biblical scholars in the practice of 'reading with', provided we have been converted 'from below'.

105. Tracy, *Plurality and Ambiguity*, p. 90.

3 |

What (Socially Engaged) Biblical Scholars Do

Experience in South Africa and Brazil in the interface constituted by 'reading with', in which the subjectivities of both socially engaged biblical scholar and poor and marginalized reader are vigilantly foregrounded and power relations are acknowledged and equalized, demonstrates the need for both 'community consciousness' and 'critical consciousness'. The experiences, questions, needs and interests as well as the readings and resources of the community, are the starting point of contextual Bible study, and socially engaged biblical scholars must allow themselves to be partially constituted by this reality.[1] But what is the place of 'critical consciousness', and, more specifically, of the critical tools which are the trade of biblical scholars—do they have a role to play?

Socially engaged biblical scholars have always accepted the parameters of the contextual Bible study process; that the Bible must be read from the perspective of the organized poor and marginalized, that the Bible must be read together with the poor and marginalized, that Bible reading is related to social transformation, and, significantly, that the Bible must be read critically. While biblical scholars differ, because they have different interpretative interests, on the modes of critical reading to be used, some favouring socio-historical modes (e.g. Itumeleng Mosala and Elisabeth Schüssler Fiorenza),[2] others literary and rhetorical modes

---

1.   Gerald O. West, 'No Integrity without Contextuality: The Presence of Particularity in Biblical Hermeneutics and Pedagogy', *Scriptura* S11 (1993), pp. 131-46 (144); Sharon D. Welch, *A Feminist Ethic of Risk* (Minneapolis: Fortress Press, 1990), p. 144.

2.   Itumeleng J. Mosala, *Biblical Hermeneutics and Black Theology in South*

(e.g. Phyllis Trible and Mieke Bal),[3] and still others symbolic, thematic, and metaphoric modes (e.g. Sandra Schneiders and J. Severino Croatto),[4] the vital similarity is that all these modes of reading offer a *critical* reading of the Bible—they ask systematic and structured sets of questions of the Bible. There is no mystery here; biblical scholars read critically because they have been trained to ask structured and systematic sets of questions in their reading practices, whether their focus be behind the text, on the text, or in front of the text.

Another important and related similarity of these different critical modes of reading is the concern that any appropriation of the Bible, whether from behind the text, in the text, or in front of the text, is a *critical appropriation*. A *critical* reading and appropriation of the biblical text is a central concern from the side of (organic) intellectuals involved in the interface between an engaged biblical studies with its socially committed trained readers of the Bible and ordinary poor and marginalized 'readers' of the Bible.[5]

Our reasons for this emphasis on critical modes of reading are related to a particular understanding of domination and resistance, as the previous chapter indicates. Shaped as most of us were by analyses that argued for strong notions of hegemony, we argued that interpreters of the Bible could no longer ignore the ideological nature of all interpretation, and indeed, of all texts, including the biblical texts. Itumeleng Mosala speaks for many when he argues that biblical texts are 'products, records, and sites of social, historical, cultural, gender, racial, and ideological struggles' and that they 'radically and indelibly bear the marks of their

Africa (Grand Rapids: Eerdmans, 1989); and Elisabeth Schüssler Fiorenza, *In Memory of Her* (London: SCM Press, 1983).

3.   Phyllis Trible, *God and the Rhetoric of Sexuality: Overtures to Biblical Theology* (Philadelphia: Fortress Press, 1978); and *idem, Texts of Terror: Literary-Feminist Readings of Biblical Narratives* (Philadelphia: Fortress Press, 1984); Mieke Bal, *Death and Dissymmetry: The Politics of Coherence in the Book of Judges* (Chicago: University of Chicago Press, 1988).

4.   Sandra M. Schneiders, 'Feminist Ideology Criticism and Biblical Hermeneutics', *Biblical Theology Bulletin* 19 (1989), pp. 3-10; and J. Severino Croatto, *Biblical Hermeneutics: Toward a Theory of Reading as the Production of Meaning* (Maryknoll, NY: Orbis Books, 1987).

5.   This is clearest in the work of Mosala, Schüssler Fiorenza and Norman K. Gottwald.

origins and history'.[6] The biblical text is not 'an innocent and transparent container of a message or messages'.[7]

While much of Latin American, African-American and Black South African biblical hermeneutics has been slow to recognize the ideological nature of the biblical text, the penetrating analyses of feminist and womanist hermeneutics indicate a fundamental shift in the debate.[8] The debate is no longer whether the biblical text is an ideological product;[9] the debate is now about what the particular ideology of a particular text is, and how (or whether) we should therefore interpret and use the Bible. The responses to such questions are many and various. They include the post-biblical response of Mary Daly,[10] the historical-materialist response of Mosala, the literary (or rhetorical) response of Phyllis Trible, and the thematic/symbolic responses of Rosemary Radford Ruether,[11] J. Severino Croatto and Sandra Schneiders.

For socially engaged biblical scholars who recognize the ideological nature of the biblical text and yet who continue to interpret and appropriate the biblical tradition, often because they are called to by the poor and marginalized, it is important to hold

6. Mosala, *Black Theology*, p. 20.
7. Mosala, *Black Theology*, p. 40.
8. Katharine Doob Sakenfeld, 'Feminist Uses of Biblical Materials', in Letty M. Russel (ed.), *Feminist Interpretations of the Bible* (Philadelphia: Westminster Press, 1985), pp. 55-64; Clarice J. Martin, 'The *Haustafeln* (Household Codes) in African American Biblical Interpretation: "Free Slaves" and "Subordinate Women"', in Cain Hope Felder (ed.), *Stony the Road We Trod: African American Biblical Interpretation* (Minneapolis: Fortress Press, 1991), pp. 206-31.
9. However, see Steven E. Fowl, 'Texts Don't Have Ideologies', *Biblical Interpretation* 3 (1995), pp. 15-34; see also Mark G. Brett, 'The Political Ethics of Postmodern Allegory', in M. Daniel Carroll R., David J.A. Clines and Philip R. Davies (eds.), *The Bible in Human Society: Essays in Honour of John Rogerson* (JSOTSup, 200; Sheffield: Sheffield Academic Press, 1995), pp. 67-86, particularly pp. 71-76.
10. Mary Daly, *Gynecology: The Metaethics of Radical Feminism* (Boston: Beacon Press, 1978). Daly seeks to move from the reading of androcentric texts to the construction of a life-centre that generates new cultural texts, traditions and mythologies. Such a move rejects both biblical texts and biblical tradition.
11. Rosemary Radford Ruether, *Sexism and God-talk: Towards a Feminist Theology* (London: SCM Press, 1983).

together both a hermeneutic of suspicion and a hermeneutic of trust. On the one hand, we want to insist that there is no innocent interpretation, no innocent interpreter, no innocent text; on the other hand, we believe that empowering and liberating interpretation of the Bible is still possible.[12] Critical modes of reading the Bible enable both.

Critical modes of reading the Bible enable ordinary 'readers' to recognize the ideological nature of the biblical text (and their context) and to develop critical tools which will enable them to do their own critical analysis of text (and context). The transfer of critical resources between their reading practice and the reality of their daily life is a central concern of socially engaged biblical scholars, particularly those who advocate socio-historical modes of reading. For some socially engaged biblical scholars, the contextual Bible study process is primarily an opportunity to practise and rehearse for the real thing—critical analysis of social reality.[13] For others, however, critical modes of reading also provide resources for a hermeneutic of engagement, connecting ordinary poor and marginalized 'readers' with the 'dangerous memories'[14] and the 'subjugated knowledges'[15] of those who have struggled for survival, liberation and life in and behind the biblical text. A hermeneutic of engagement emphasizes both accountability to present communities of faith and struggle, by accepting that the Bible is a significant text for them, and continuity with past poor and marginalized communities of faith and struggle, by not abandoning their traces in the Bible.[16] Recognizing the damage done by the Bible, socially engaged biblical scholars insist on critical modes of reading; recognizing that the Bible still possesses the power to orient life in a meaningful, truthful, powerful way,[17] socially engaged biblical scholars insist on a critical appropriation.

---

12. See Tracy, *Plurality and Ambiguity*.

13. Part of Mosala's work gives this impression.

14. Johann Baptist Metz, *Faith in History and Society: Toward a Practical Fundamental Theology* (London: Burns and Oates, 1980).

15. Welch, *A Feminist Ethic*.

16. Schüssler Fiorenza, *In Memory*, p. xix.

17. Linell E. Cady, 'Hermeneutics and Tradition: The Role of the Past in Jurisprudence and Theology', *Harvard Theological Journal* 79 (1986), pp. 439-63 (455-58).

Different socially engaged biblical scholars will make different judgments about the potential resources of the Bible to orient human life in a meaningful, truthful and powerful way,[18] but most accept the argument that insofar as the Bible is still influential today and insofar as it forms a significant part of the personal, cultural and religious reality of poor and marginalized communities, we have to engage critically with it. 'We will either transform it into a new liberating future or continue to be subject to its tyranny whether we recognize its power or not.'[19] Furthermore, some socially engaged biblical scholars would argue that many of the emerging modes of reading within biblical scholarship offer formidable resources for recovering forgotten, neglected and absent voices, so that it is precisely at this moment that biblical scholarship has something substantial to offer to those who would probe the boundaries, gaps, and cracks of the Bible. Drawing on such resources Schüssler Fiorenza seeks to assist women in reclaiming early Christian history 'as women's own past' and as 'an integral part of early Christian historiography' and in locating and standing in solidarity with the memories of suffering and hope of their foresisters.[20] Similarly, using such resources

18. Cady, 'Hermeneutics and Tradition', pp. 460-61.

19. Schüssler Fiorenza, *In Memory*, p. xix. Similarly, Ruether argues that to express contemporary experience in a cultural and historical vacuum is both 'self-deluding and unsatisfying'. 'It is self-deluding because to communicate at all to oneself and others, one makes use of patterns of thought, however transformed by new experience, that have a history. It is unsatisfactory because, however much one discards large historical periods of dominant traditions, one still seeks to encompass this "fallen history" within a larger context of authentic and truthful life. To look back to some original base of meaning and truth before corruption is to know that truth is more basic than falsehood and hence able, ultimately, to root out falsehood in a new future that is dawning in contemporary experience. To find glimmers of this truth in submerged and alternative traditions through history is to assure oneself that one is not mad or duped. Only by finding an alternative historical community and tradition more deeply rooted than those that have become corrupted can one feel sure that in criticizing the dominant tradition one is not just subjectively criticizing the dominant tradition but is, rather, touching a deeper bedrock of authentic Being upon which to ground the self. One cannot wield the lever of criticism without a place to stand' (Ruether, *Sexism*, p. 18).

20. Schüssler Fiorenza, *In Memory*, pp. xix-xx.

Takatso Mofokeng enables black Christians, 'as members of a silenced, marginalized and sometimes ignored race' to discover 'the silenced, ignored and marginalized people in the Bible and develop an affinity with them' and as 'a text that has been silenced but one that speaks through this silence about the struggles of the silenced and marginalized people of the Bible'.[21] Such discoveries constitute 'the liberation of the Bible from the clutches of the dominant in the Christian fold who impose the stories that justify their victories onto the oppressed'.[22]

It is clear from this discussion that critical modes of reading and appropriation, and these moments cannot be separated,[23] are integrally related to the emancipatory concerns of socially engaged biblical scholars. The socially engaged biblical scholar, what Osayande Obery Hendricks calls 'the guerrilla exegete', is not primarily concerned about the acclaim or the claim of the academy, she or he does not wait for 'the hegemonic pat on the head'.

> No, s/he struggles because her/his people are bibliocentric, their lives devotedly focused on a Bible whose liberatory power has been defused and confused by dominationist interpreters. S/he struggles for the lives of those lovingly dedicated to a Bible whose strategically imposed hegemonic readings militate against their own fragile well-being. S/he struggles because the Bible continues to stand as the foremost tool of oppression and hegemonic domination in human history, surpassing even the *Communist Manifesto* for the mayhem committed in its name. Used to justify slavery. Lynching. Segregation. Genocide. Rampant militarism. Gender oppression. Myriad exclusions. A full calendar of hurts. Flawless flesh declared leprous. Beautiful hearts declared impure. A gospel of liberation debauched to a rationale for oppression. A proclamation of freedom perverted to promulgation of dominationist rhetorics. A chill-pill for the outraged. The balm in Gilead become social novocaine and priestly poison.[24]

21. Takatso Mofokeng, 'Black Christians, the Bible and Liberation', *The Journal of Black Theology* 2 (1988), pp. 34-42 (41).

22. Mofokeng, 'Black Christians', p. 41.

23. See Hans-Georg Gadamer, *Truth and Method* (New York: Seabury, 1975).

24. Hendricks, 'Guerilla Exegesis', p. 82.

What then is the relationship between the interpretative interests and the social interests of the socially engaged biblical scholar? Biblical scholars have a range of what can helpfully be called interpretative interests. In order to bring some clarity into discussions about textual interpretation Jeffrey Stout proposes that we use a form of Quinean explication with regard to the problematic term 'meaning'. Explication can be seen 'as a means for exchanging more troublesome for less troublesome terms. Good explications…tell us how to translate theories from familiar but confusing idioms into idioms better suited to our purposes.'[25]

What, then, might our concerns be when we inquire about the meaning of a text? We might, for example, be interested in the author's intentions in a text, or in the narrative shape of a text, or in the symbolic trajectories of a group of texts, or in the text as a product of a particular mode of production. So, then, we can replace the term 'meaning' with the term 'interpretative interest'. While different uses of the term 'meaning' in Biblical Studies, for example, 'all bear in one way or another on the interpretation of texts', they do not, Stout argues, 'pick out the same aspect or feature of texts as the common topic for inquiry'. 'Interpretative interest' points to what 'meaning' hides.[26] Explicating 'meaning' in terms of interpretative interests reveals that some of our most intractable disagreements about textual meaning are not really disagreements about the same thing. What we thought to be one topic is really several topics.[27] So Stout's proposal is that we dissolve disputes about the meaning of texts by explicating these disputes in terms of interpretative interests.[28]

25. Jeffery Stout, 'What Is the Meaning of a Text?', *New Literary History* 14 (1982), pp. 1-12 (2).

26. Stout, 'What Is the Meaning of a Text?', p. 6.

27. Stephen E. Fowl, 'The Ethics of Interpretation or What's Left Over after the Elimination of Meaning', in David J.A. Clines, Stephen E. Fowl and Stanley E. Porter (eds.), *The Bible in Three Dimensions: Essays in Celebration of Forty Years of Biblical Studies in the University of Sheffield* (JSOTSup, 87; Sheffield: Sheffield Academic Press, 1990), pp. 379-98 (385).

28. See also S. Mailloux, 'Rhetorical Hermeneutics', *Critical Inquiry* 11 (1985), pp. 620-41; and Richard Rorty, 'Texts and Lumps', *New Literary History* 17 (1985), pp. 1-16.

This analysis is helpful in clarifying the plurality of interpretative interests that constitute the terrain of biblical scholarship. This analysis also enables us to distinguish, and so to explore the relationship, between what I have called social interests and interpretative interests. Social interests include those factors that make and mark us as people. While our selves are constituted by a multiplicity of organisms, institutions, forces, energies, materials, desires, thoughts and practices, we can identify those factors that substantially and indelibly inscribe us. And if we are reluctant to do this, others will do it for us! Aspects of our selves that impinge on others can be readily identified and described by them. The readiness of others to name us has opened the way for biblical scholars to be more honest about who they are and what their social interests are,[29] though some still pretend to have no social interests at all as they interpret. Various forms of reader-response criticism and autobiographical criticism have helpfully acknowledged the social interests of the biblical scholar.[30] Generally, however, while most biblical scholars are fairly overt about their interpretative interests, even if they do not reflect analytically on them, they are usually much more covert about their social interests.

Fortunately, the advocacy stance of socially engaged biblical scholars foregrounds social interests, and so one is able to examine the relationship between their interpretative and social interests. Biblical scholars who are called by the poor and marginalized to read the Bible with them tend, as I have indicated, to be those who collaborate and stand in solidarity with them as they struggle for survival, liberation and life. They also tend to be those who, for a variety of reasons, find some form of continuity with the biblical tradition, though this is usually in places at its boundaries, margins and edges. This being the case, their interpretative interests shape the form that this continuity takes. Those, like Mosala

29. See, for example, Daniel Patte and Gary Phillips, 'A Fundamental Condition for Ethical Accountability in the Teaching of the Bible by White Male Exegetes: Recovering and Claiming the Specificity of our Perspective', *Scriptura* S9 (1992), pp. 7-28.

30. See the essays in Janice Capel Anderson and Jeffrey L. Staley (eds.), *Taking It Personally: Autobiographical Biblical Criticism* (Semeia, 72; Atlanta: Scholars Press, 1995).

and Schüssler Fiorenza, who have interpretative interests in the socio-historical dimensions of the text emphasize continuity with sectors and sites of struggle in the reconstructed societies behind the text. Similarly, those with various types of literary interests concentrate on continuity with elements of the text itself, using a range of resources to read the text carefully and closely and to probe for cracks, traces and absences in the text.

The social interests of socially engaged biblical scholars, partially constituted as they are by their solidarity with the poor and marginalized, shape the questions that they bring to the biblical text, but they do not necessarily determine their interpretative interests. So, for example, biblical scholars in solidarity with the struggle of women will bring the experiences, needs, questions and resources of women to the the Bible, but they do this differently. Schüssler Fiorenza reconstructs the social reality of first-century women,[31] Trible tells untold tales of textual terror in which women are victims,[32] and Schneiders inhabits the world of God's project of liberation for women in front of the text.[33]

Some socially engaged scholars claim that certain interpretative interests ought to be adopted in the process of 'reading with' ordinary poor and marginalized communities and so would want to privilege their particular reading methodology. This point of view is most common among socially engaged biblical scholars with socio-historical interpretative interests, and has two prongs to it. First, both Mosala and Schüssler Fiorenza, for example, insist that socio-historical concerns are required in struggles for survival, liberation and life because they are non-selective, in that all texts are analysed as social products of particular social systems and struggles. Other interpretative interests that do not give priority to socio-historical concerns, they argue, are in danger of producing uncritical and unstructural understandings of the Bible, which simply reinforce and confirm uncritical and unstructural understandings of present social struggles and systems. As the final phrase in this sentence indicates, the second prong of their

31. Schüssler Fiorenza, *In Memory*; see West, *Biblical Hermeneutics*, pp. 140-46.

32. Trible, *Texts of Terror*; see West, *Biblical Hermeneutics*, pp. 146-54.

33. Schneiders, *Feminist Ideology Criticism*; see West, *Biblical Hermeneutics*, pp. 154-62, particularly n. 191.

argument has to do with the transfer of analytical resources from the reading of the Bible to the reading of context.[34]

Selective readings of the Bible are definitely problematic for socially engaged biblical scholars, and smack of forms of fundamentalism, whether of the Right or Left. However, in characterizing 'on the text' and 'in front of the text' modes of reading as selective, uncritical, and unstructural, Mosala and Schüssler Fiorenza, to stay with the example, misunderstand these modes of reading and therefore their contribution. The second concern which calls for the transfer of skills and concepts for social analysis from the reading process is more substantial, but places too much weight on the particular analytical resources of socio-historical approaches, minimizing the many resources that other modes of reading offer. Furthermore, by operating within a model of domination and resistance that has been questioned in the previous chapter, the critical resources of the scholar are over-emphasized, minimizing the critical contribution and resources of the ordinary poor and marginalized 'reader'. Finally, we must remember that our interpretative interests are not only shaped by our solidarity with the social interests of the poor and marginalized communities that partially constitute their experience, but also by the interpretative interests that constitute the scholarly communities in which we were trained and in which we are situated. They do not self-evidently arise from the site of struggle itself, no matter how appropriate to that struggle they may seem. For these reasons, then, we should not privilege these particular interpretative interests over others.

The range of critical resources of socially engaged biblical scholars are potentially empowering in communities of the poor and marginalized, both in their capacity to analyse the biblical text and the social context of the interpreter. But this is not, I have come to see, their primary contribution. What is really useful about our critical contributions to the reading process is the various forms of continuity with (aspects of) the biblical tradition they facilitate, whatever the mode of reading used. This is, after all, what biblical scholars do, as I will now show.

---

34. For example Schüssler Fiorenza, *In Memory*, and Mosala, *Black Theology*; see West, *Biblical Hermeneutics*, pp. 135-73.

What are biblical scholars doing when they read the Bible? This is a complex and difficult question to answer, but we can begin to approach an answer by briefly examining a particular case of a socially engaged biblical scholar reading. Carol Meyers, for instance, is interested in a detailed historical and sociological reconstruction of the society behind the biblical text and of the life of women in such a society. In order to accomplish this task an interdisciplinary approach including feminist scholarship and social scientific (mainly sociological, anthropological and archaeological) research is used.[35]

Beginning with social interests rooted in the experienced reality and identities of particular women, Meyers recognizes that the Bible 'as a source presents problems of omission in its treatment of women as individuals or as a group. Its androcentric bias and also its urban, elite orientation mean that even the information it contains may be a distortion or misrepresentation of the lives of women removed from urban centers and bureaucratic families'.[36] However, a 'behind the text' reading recovers the average Israelite woman, who is neither named nor described in the biblical text.

In her readings, Meyers concentrates on the premonarchic period for two reasons: first, it is the period of Israelite existence which is best known in terms of its social configurations, and second, it is the formative era in the long story of the biblical people.[37] Her detailed and careful reconstructions of the life of ordinary women in this period echo elements of Scott's analysis and lead her to conclude that while

> incipient gender hierarchies may have existed even in earliest Israel and were certainly present in the monarchic period,... female power deriving from the various roles (economic and other) played by women in the complex peasant households enabled them to minimize or offset whatever formal authority was held by males. Assumptions of male dominance and female

35. This does not mean that Meyers pays no attention to literary aspects of the text; quite to the contrary, Meyers demonstrates considerable sensitivity to the literary dimensions of the text (see Carol Meyers, *Discovering Eve: Ancient Israelite Women in Context* [Oxford: Oxford University Press, 1988], Chs. 4–5).

36. Meyers, *Discovering Eve*, pp. 13-14.

37. Meyers, *Discovering Eve*, p. 14.

subservience in ancient Israel, derived from formal texts and from
postbiblical traditions, may be part of the 'myth' of male control
masking a situation of male dependence.[38]

Foregrounding her reading method, Meyers argues that because gender relationships 'are the consequence of complex influ-
ences, involving specific social and economic arrangements',
reconstructing the internal dynamics of a society 'is the only
legitimate way to dispel the "myth" and to increase the visibility of
Eve'. Her reading practice 'allows us to see Eve as a figure no less
powerful than her male counterpart'.[39]

What Meyers does is clear. In the Bible, which is the ideological
record of particular sectors of ancient Israel, we glimpse traces of
the lives of powerful ordinary women.[40] But their lives can only be
rediscovered and reclaimed by reading behind the text. What this
mode of reading reveals is a picture of ordinary women in their
context. Meyers continually makes the point that understanding
biblical texts requires that we interpret them from the perspective
of their ancient context and not from the perspective of our
modern context, and in this respect she shares the concerns of
Mosala and Schüssler Fiorenza discussed a few pages above.
Understanding the contextual reality of the early Israelites,
particularly the social reality of Israelite women, is thus 'central to
interpreting the original message and function' of a particular
text.[41]

Many biblical scholars go no further than this, at least not
overtly. They stop, it appears, with what the text meant. We know
well the tried, and tired, distinction between exegesis ('what it
meant') and interpretation ('what it means'), and the claim of
most 'serious' biblical scholars that their task is the former. But
those who have been the victims of 'exegesis' know that there is
no innocent interpreter; they know that social interests lurk below
the surface of 'neutrality' and 'objectivity'.[42] Carol Meyers as a

38. Meyers, *Discovering Eve*, p. 181.
39. Meyers, *Discovering Eve*, p. 181.
40. Meyers, *Discovering Eve*, p. 71.
41. Meyers, *Discovering Eve*, pp. 93, 120.
42. Keith W. Whitelam, *The Invention of Ancient Israel: The Silencing of
Palestinian History* (New York: Routledge, 1996). This work is a devastating
critique of 'the hidden transcript' (agenda) of biblical scholarship.

socially engaged biblical scholar is more honest, and so she asks, overtly, what her reading might mean for women's struggles today. Her answer, we must note, has to do both with the reading process and product.

> If the egalitarian values and patterns that prevailed during those prestate centuries are to have any meaning for later generations, including our own, this recovery of Everywoman Eve's life and context should make the nonhierarchical position of women a visible and enduring model, as are the other widely acclaimed theological and social innovations and accomplishments, of early Israel.[43]

As this final comment indicates, other scholars too have found 'visible and enduring models' for present communities in past biblical sources. Norman Gottwald is one such scholar, who, from a slightly different angle, argues that as socio-historical study of the origins of Israel

> penetrates more and more deeply to the circumstances and dynamics of Yahwism's emergence, the integral social-revolutionary character of Yahwism comes more clearly to light and thereby once again challenges the synagogues and churches with the disturbing implications and consequences of claiming continuity with a religion sprung from such roots.[44]

For Meyers biblical sources provide useful reading resources, both in terms of reading process and reading product, for women today who are struggling against oppression and marginalization and who choose to stay in continuity with the biblical tradition. For Gottwald biblical sources provide a challenge to those who claim to be in continuity with the biblical tradition but who participate in and perpetuate systems of domination.[45] For both scholars, biblical sources are a resource for present communities who have some form of continuity with the biblical tradition.

We know that it is not only scholars who re-use biblical sources as resources. Although they do it differently, and I will examine this difference in the next chapter, ordinary 'readers' of the Bible use biblical sources regularly to construct the 'working' readings

43. Meyers, *Discovering Eve*, p. 188.
44. Norman K. Gottwald, *The Tribes of Yahweh: A Sociology of the Religion of Liberated Israel, 1250–1050 BC* (Maryknoll, NY: Orbis Books, 1979), p. 597.
45. Each would also support the emphasis of the other.

and theologies that they live by. This process of re-using received sources is also a part of the biblical tradition itself. There are many examples, but a readily recognizable one is 'the exodus'. Gottwald charts an early occurrence of 'exodus' sources, what he calls 'the Moses traditions', being of use to the newly emerging Israelite society in Canaan.

> The full dimensions of the socioreligious attraction of the Moses traditions for the confederacy of Israel...has to be explained with reference to lines of connection drawn between the *critical problems* faced by the Moses group and by later Israel and with reference to the lines of connection between the *socioreligious strategies* for coping with those problems developed respectively by the earlier migratory and later sedentary communities.[46]

These earliest of sources, comprising a religio-political contract or covenant, socio-economic and ritual laws, and God-as-Yahweh, become resources for subsequent communities, and in the process are taken up into other more familiar sources (e.g. J, E, D and P), which in turn are used again and again in various forms by communities in continuity with these traditions, including Mark's New Testament community,[47] and present communities in many contexts, perhaps even for us in South Africa with our Reconstruction and Development Programme (RDP),[48] whenever 'lines of connection' can be found. This is the thrust of my argument in this chapter: critically discerning *lines of connection* between biblical traditions, like J, E, D, P, and present realities facing poor and marginalized communities, like the RDP in South Africa, seems to

---

46. Norman K. Gottwald, *The Hebrew Bible: A Socio-literary Introduction* (Philadelphia: Fortress Press, 1985), p. 225.

47. See Jonathan A. Draper, 'Wandering Radicalism or Purposeful Activity? Jesus and the Sending of Messengers in Mark 6.6-56', *Neotestamentica* 29 (1995), pp. 187-207.

48. 'The RDP is an instrument for transforming government and society. It is intended to make government more transparent and accountable to the people. It also transforms society to take the leading role and responsibility for their own development in the process of reconstructing South Africa. The RDP is an integrated programme, based on people, that will provide peace and security for all and build a nation. It links reconstruction and development and deepens democracy—these are the basic principles of the RDP' (from an information brochure issued by the Minister without Portfolio, 21 September 1994).

be what socially engaged biblical scholars do; they locate links between J, E, D, P and the RDP!

Indeed, this is what all biblical scholars do: they trace *lines of connection* between biblical texts and between biblical texts and other ancient texts; they also trace *lines of connection* between biblical texts and the worlds that produced them. Socially engaged biblical scholars go further by overtly tracing *lines of connection* between biblical texts and contexts and the texts and contexts of present communities of the poor and marginalized. In the case of Mosala, for example, this involves using historical-critical and sociological, specifically historical-materialist, tools in order to identify those layers or sources that are the products of the oppressed classes. Trible uses the resources of a literary approach—the rhetorical formation of sentences, episodes and scenes, as well as overall design and plot structure, and the portrayal of characters[49]—to uncover a counter-literature of neglected themes and untold tales. By understanding the text 'as a mediation of meaning that takes place as event in the reader',[50] Schneiders decontextualizes and then recontextualizes the text by bringing different experiences and questions to the reading process and in so doing is invited to inhabit a symbolic structure with a surplus of meaning. Whether their interpretative interests take them behind the text, into the text, or in front of the text, they all trace *lines of connection* between aspects of the text and the realities of present communities with which they collaborate in projects of survival, liberation and life.

As I have already argued, socially engaged biblical scholars are probably more aware than most that the Bible is no innocent text. Mosala, for example, argues that biblical scholars 'have always been aware of the tendency in biblical literature to use older traditions to address the needs of new situations', but that they have not always recognized the ideological agendas of the dominant classes that usually direct the new usage.[51] From her literary perspective Trible makes a similar point, stressing that 'the patriarchal stamp of scripture is permanent'.[52] And the in front of the

49. Trible, *Texts of Terror*, pp. 3-4.
50. Schneiders, 'Feminist Ideology Criticism', p. 5.
51. Mosala, *Black Theology*, p. 101.
52. Trible, *God and the Rhetoric*, p. 202.

text readings of Schneiders too confront 'the oppressiveness in the text'.[53] Consequently, continuity—lines of connection—with the biblical tradition is no easy matter. But because biblical texts have continuing effects and because the biblical tradition is in some sense still meaningful, powerful and true for many members of poor and marginalized communities, the reading tools, strategies and products of biblical scholarship are potentially useful in providing different ways of locating lines of connection with the biblical tradition which resonate with their 'working' theologies and 'readings'. Ordinary 'readers' have their own ways of doing this, as the next chapter demonstrates, but readily take up other additional resources when they are offered. Received readings, reflecting the social interests of missionaries, ecclesiastical hierarchies, and other dominant sectors, offer little to live by, so poor and marginalized 'readers' must look in unlikely places and use unusual devices to forage for and forge lines of connection between the God of life who is with them in their daily struggles and the biblical tradition as it has been proclaimed to them. This is no easy matter, but ordinary 'readers' are remarkably resourceful, as we see in the next chapter.

---

53. Schneiders, 'Feminist Ideology Criticism', p. 9.

4 |

'Re-membering' the Bible:
The Other Does Speak

Before I chart the contours of the reading practices and resources of 'the other' and probe the place of the socially engaged biblical scholar in relation to these strategies and resources, I would like to be more specific about the limits of my discussion. So I must begin by numbering and naming 'the other' who is the specific subject of my discourse. Ordinary African 'readers' of the Bible from poor and marginalized communities in South Africa constitute 'the other' I read with. There is something of the slogan in this formulation, and I acknowledge its imprecision. But slogans have their place, even in academic reflection, and the indeterminate designation reminds us of the shifting boundaries that constitute this 'other'. The slowly changing socio-economic profile of the South African population and the constellations of forces and factors that currently shape our subjectivities reconstitute who this 'other' is from day to day.

I do not want to qualify my comments concerning 'the ordinary African "reader" of the Bible from poor and marginalized communities' much further, except to make it quite clear that my reflections arise from work in very specific and actual communities. Each of these communities could be surveyed and categorized sociologically, and in much of my work I have attempted to provide a profile of who I am reading with in each particular case.[1] However, here in this chapter I reflect more generally

---

1. Gerald O. West, 'And the Dumb Do Speak: Articulating Incipient Readings of the Bible in Marginalised Communities', in John W. Rogerson, Margaret Davies and M. Daniel Carroll R. (eds.), *The Bible in Ethics: The Second Sheffield Colloquium* (JSOTSup, 207; Sheffield: Sheffield Academic Press, 1995), pp. 174-92, and Gerald O. West, 'The Interface between Trained Readers

across these communities on the reading resources and strategies I and others have encountered there. One more observation is appropriate concerning these 'others'; they are the most 'other'[2] and they are numerically the most—they are the majority of 'readers' of the Bible in South Africa.

Before I come to a more empirical exploration of the reading strategies and resources of 'the others' it may be instructive to approach the subject from an historical perspective. In the Preface to their study of the colonization of consciousness and the consciousness of colonization in South Africa among the Southern Tswana people, Jean and John Comaroff tell the story of how in 1818 the directors of the London Missionary Society sent a mechanical clock to the church at its first mission station among the Tswana. As the Comaroffs remark, this was no ordinary clock for two related reasons. First, the clock was peculiar in that the hours of the clock were struck by marching British soldiers carved of wood. Second, the clock represented 'the measure of a historical process in the making'.

> Clearly meant to proclaim the value of time in Christian, civilized communities, the contraption had an altogether unexpected impact. For the Africans insisted that the 'carved ones' were emissaries of a distant king who, with missionary connivance, would place them in a 'house of bondage.' A disconsolate evangelist had eventually to 'take down the fairy-looking strangers, and cut a piece off their painted bodies, to convince the affrighted natives that the objects of their alarm were only bits of coloured wood'.[3]

However, the Tswana were not reassured; 'indeed, they seem to have concluded that "the motives of the missionary were anything but disinterested." And they were correct, of course. In the face of the clock they had caught their first glimpse of a future time, a time when their colonized world would march to quite different rhythms.'[4]

While the Comaroffs chart the coming of the imperial clock and trace the processes by which non-conformist Christian mis-

and Ordinary Readers in Liberation Hermeneutics—A Case Study: Mark 10.17-22', *Neotestamentica* 27 (1993), pp. 165-80.

   2.   Tracy, *Plurality and Ambiguity*, pp. 72, 90, 100-104, 141.
   3.   Comaroff and Comaroff, *Of Revelation and Revolution*, p. xi.
   4.   Comaroff and Comaroff, *Of Revelation and Revolution*, p. xi.

sionaries, among the earliest footsoldiers of British colonialism, sought to change the hearts and minds, the signs and practices, of the Southern Tswana, they do not analyse the arrival and reception of the Bible as a particular colonial icon.[5]

An important task awaiting an African biblical hermeneutics is a comprehensive account of the transactions that constitute the history of the encounters between Africa and the Bible. While the accounts we have of the encounters between Africa and Christianity are well documented, the encounters between Africa and *the Bible* are partial and fragmentary. That the Bible is seldom treated separately from the arrival and reception of Christianity is not surprising, particularly as it can be argued that the Bible is analytically bound up with being a Christian.[6] I do not want to dispute the interconnectedness of the Bible and Christianity, but I do want analyse the nature of the interconnectness more carefully. We should not assume, for example, that the reception of Christianity and the reception of the Bible always amount to the same thing. Vincent Wimbush's interpretative history of the Bible among African Americans provides compelling reasons for analysing the reception of the Bible as distinct from but related to the reception of Christianity. And, writing from the Kenya context, Nahashon Ndungu notes that when the Akurinu Church emerged among the Gikuyu in Kenya there was a deliberate rejection of the beliefs and practices of the mission churches and a turn to the Bible, from which they identified their own teachings and practices.[7] But analyses like these of Wimbush and Ndungu are scarce.

Historical accounts of the encounters between Christianity and Africa are rich and detailed in their analysis of most aspects of these transactions, but consistently exclude the Bible. This is the case in the otherwise excellent recent work by Elizabeth Isichei, *A*

---

5.   My focus, like that of the Comaroffs, is on the colonial and post-colonial period. For the presence and place of the Bible in pre-colonial Africa see Ype Schaaf, *On their Way Rejoicing: The History and Role of the Bible in Africa* (Carlisle: Paternoster Press, 1994).

6.   James Barr, *Explorations in Theology*. VII. *The Scope and Authority of the Bible* (London: SCM Press, 1980), p. 52.

7.   Nahashon Ndungu, 'The Bible in an African Independent Church', in Hannah W. Kinoti and John M. Waliggo (eds.), *The Bible in African Christianity* (Nairobi: Acton Publishers, 1997), pp. 58-67 (61-62).

History of Christianity in Africa: From Antiquity to the Present,[8] where the historical, sociological, geographical, cultural, economic and religious dimensions of, for example, the emergence of North African Judaism centuries before Christ and then Christianity in the beginning of the first century, the initial interface between Judaism/Christianity and Islam, the impact of Portuguese (Catholic and Protestant) evangelization and exploitation between 1500–1800, the nineteenth-century missionaries and colonialists, and the expansion of Christianity through African evangelists in the twentieth century are all described and analysed in detail, but the biblical and hermeneutical are hardly mentioned. Even Ype Schaaf's book, subtitled *The History and Role of the Bible in Africa,* provides little analysis of the Bible's interpretative history in Africa. Much is implicit, as with the work of Isichei, but explicit analysis is absent. Though Schaaf deals with the topic of translation of the Bible in great detail, this discussion does not lead into any inventory of its interpretative history. That task still remains.

Fortunately, we do have the suggestive interpretative history of the transaction between the Bible and African Americans constructed by Wimbush, mentioned earlier. Wimbush proposes five major types of readings of the Bible among African Americans. Wimbush's research has a hermeneutical and a historical dimension in that he correlates each major type of reading with a particular historical period. His research identifies, delineates and analyses the major types of African American readings of the Bible from slavery to the present.[9] While there are many significant differences between African American transactions with the Bible and indigenous African transactions with the Bible, there are also many striking similarities which make Wimbush's analysis heuristically valuable.[10] The existing African analyses tend to sketch the terrain rather than analyse it in detail, and so I draw

8.   Elizabeth Isichei, *A History of Christianity in Africa: From Antiquity to the Present* (Grand Rapids: Eerdmans, 1995).

9.   Vincent L. Wimbush, 'The Bible and African Americans: An Outline of an Interpretative History', in Cain Hope Felder (ed.), *Stony the Road We Trod: African American Biblical Interpretation* (Minneapolis: Fortress Press, 1991), pp. 81-97 (84).

10. In addition to the discussion below, I have discussed some of these similarities in Gerald O. West, 'Re-membering the Bible in South Africa: Reading Strategies in a Postcolonial Context', *Jian Dao* 8 (1997), pp. 37-62.

here on Wimbush's account heuristically, in an attempt to trace and to analyse some of the interpretative strategies indigenous (black) South Africans have adopted in their transactions with the Bible throughout the colonial encounter and into our present postcolonial, post-apartheid and increasingly globalized context.

An analysis of the transactions between Africa and Bible, particularly the early encounters, is not only of historical value. If Wimbush is right in asserting that the array of interpretative strategies forged in the earliest encounters of African Americans with the Bible are foundational in that all other African American readings are in some sense built upon and judged by them, then such analysis has tremendous hermeneutical significance for our current context. The early African American encounters with the Bible have functioned, according to Wimbush, 'as phenomenological, socio-political and cultural foundation' for subsequent periods.[11]

African slaves' initial encounter with the Bible is characterized, according to Wimbush, by a combination of rejection, suspicion and awe of 'Book Religion'.[12] During this period the story of European colonization and conquest of 'the New World' is remarkably similar to that of their colonization and conquest of South Africa.

> They conquered native peoples and declared that European customs, languages, and traditions were the law. The Europeans' embrace of the Bible helped to lend this process legitimacy. Since many of them through their reading of and reference to the Bible had already defined themselves as dissenters from the dominant social, political, and religious traditions in their native countries, they found it a rather natural resource in the context of the New World. The Bible functioned as a cultural image-reflector, as a road map to nation-building. It provided the Europeans justification to think of themselves as a 'biblical nation,' as God's people called to conquer and convert the New World to God's way as they interpreted it.[13]

11. Vincent L. Wimbush, 'Reading Texts through Worlds, Worlds through Texts', *Semeia* 62 (1993), pp. 129-40 (131).

12. For a similar, albeit brief, account of the Bible's arrival in Africa see Mary N. Getui, 'The Bible as a Tool for Ecumenism', in Hannah W. Kinoti and John M. Waliggo (eds.), *The Bible in African Christianity* (Nairobi: Acton Publishers), pp. 86-98 (94).

13. Wimbush, 'The Bible and African Americans', p. 84.

While the Bible did play a role in the missionizing of African slaves, in the earliest encounters its role was not primary and so its impact was indirect. 'It was often imbedded within catechetical materials or within elaborate doctrinal statements and formal preaching styles.'[14] When African slaves did encounter the Bible it was from the perspective of cultures steeped in oral tradition. From this perspective the concept of religion and religious power circumscribed by a book was 'at first frightful and absurd, there-after…awesome and fascinating'.[15] As illiterate peoples with rich, well-established and elaborate oral traditions the majority of the first African slaves were suspicious of and usually rejected 'Book Religion'. However, as Wimbush notes, '[i]t did not take them long to associate the Book of "Book religion" with power'.[16] So early in their encounter with 'the Book', before they began to appropriate the Bible in an empowering and affirmative manner, their 'capacity and willingness to engage "the Book" were signifi-cant, for they demonstrated the ability of African slaves to adapt themselves to different understandings of reality', and so to survive.[17]

During what Wimbush classifies as the second period of en-counter with the Bible, African slaves began to appropriate and own the Bible. With the growth of the non-establishment, evan-gelical, camp meeting revivalist movements Africans 'began to encounter the Bible on a large and popular scale'. As significant numbers of Africans converted to Christianity, even establishing their own churches and denominational groups, they began to embrace the Bible.

> What did not go unnoticed among the Africans was the fact that the white world they experienced tended to explain its power and authority by appeal to the Bible. So they embraced the Bible, transforming it from the book of the religion of whites—whether aristocratic slavers or lower class exhorters—into a source of (psy-chic-spiritual) power, a source of inspiration for learning and affirmation, and into a language world of strong hopes and veiled but stinging critique of slave-holding Christian culture.[18]

14. Wimbush, 'Reading Texts', p. 130.
15. Wimbush, 'Reading Texts', p. 131.
16. Wimbush, 'The Bible and African Americans', p. 85.
17. Wimbush, 'The Bible and African Americans', p. 85.
18. Wimbush, 'Reading Texts', p. 131.

The point Wimbush is making here is that African slaves, like their conquered and colonized cousins in Africa, learned, appropriated, adapted and added to the hermeneutic moves of the European 'masters'. African slaves would have noted the diversity of readings the Bible could inspire, including cultural, political and denominational (religious) readings. They would also have observed the selective way in which the missionaries and preachers read the Bible; they read certain parts and ignored others. The various forms in which readings of the Bible could be articulated were appropriated and amplified: 'in song, prayers, sermons, testimonies, and addresses'.[19] If the missionaries and masters could interpret the 'the Book' under the guidance of the Spirit, then so could they.

> And interpret they did. They were attracted primarily to the narratives of the Hebrew Bible dealing with the adventures of the Hebrews in bondage and escaping from bondage, to the oracles of the eighth-century prophets and their denunciations of social injustice and visions of social justice, and to the New Testament texts concerning the compassion, passion, and resurrection of Jesus. With these and other texts, the African American Christians laid the foundations for what can be seen as an emerging 'canon'. In their spirituals and in their sermons and testimonies African Americans interpreted the Bible in the light of their experiences. Faith became indentification with the heroes and heroines of the Hebrew Bible and with the long-suffering but ultimately victorious Jesus. As the people of God in the Hebrew Bible were once delivered from enslavement, so, the Africans sang and shouted, would they be delivered. As Jesus suffered unjustly but was raised from the dead to new life, so, they sang, would they be 'raised' from their 'social death' to new life. So went the songs, sermons, and testimonies.[20]

These various forms—spirituals, sermons and testimonies—embody the hermeneutical processes whereby African slaves appropriated the Bible as their own property. They 'reflect a hermeneutic characterized by a looseness, even playfulness, vis-à-vis the biblical texts themselves'. Wimbush goes on to offer a fuller description of this 'looseness' and 'playfulness'.[21] A looseness and playfulness towards the text includes the following

19. Wimbush, 'The Bible and African Americans', p. 86.
20. Wimbush, 'The Bible and African Americans', pp. 86-87.
21. Wimbush, 'The Bible and African Americans', pp. 88-89.

strategies: interpretation 'was not controlled by the literal words of the texts, but by social experience'; texts were heard and retold more than read; texts 'were engaged as stories that seized and freed the imagination'; biblical texts were usually interpreted collectively; biblical stories 'functioned sometimes as allegory, as parable, or as veiled social criticism' in a situation where survival demanded disguised forms of resisting discourse; certain texts in the canon were read and others ignored.

In addition to offering a preliminary description of these formative hermeneutical processes, Wimbush also wants to argue that the array of interpretative strategies forged in this period of African American encounter with the Bible are foundational: all other readings would in some sense be built upon and judged by them. The beginning of the African American encounter with the Bible has functioned, according to Wimbush, 'as phenomenological, socio-political and cultural foundation' for subsequent periods.[22] The Bible, understood as 'the white folk's book', 'was accepted but not interpreted in the way that white Christians and the dominant culture in general interpreted it'.[23]

In the absence of a careful analysis and history of the early encounters of indigenous South Africans with the Bible, the first two phases of Wimbush's interpretative history are suggestive, especially in two respects. His characterization of the hermeneutics of encounter as 'a looseness, even playfulness' towards the biblical text and his claim that such a hermeneutics is foundational for and constitutive of the hermeneutics of subsequent phases in the ongoing encounter with the Bible are particularly insightful and significant, and resonate with my own research and reflections on the South African context, and finds echoes in the work of some South African Black theologians.

As we have seen, the encounter between indigenous South Africans and the Bible is usually recounted by South African Black theologians in broad strokes: 'When the white man came to our country he had the Bible and we had the land. The white man said to us "let us pray". After the prayer, the white man had the

---

22. Wimbush, 'Reading Texts', p. 131.
23. Wimbush, 'The Bible and African Americans', p. 89. See also my discussion of the work of Lamin Sanneh and Kwame Bediako below.

land and we had the Bible.'[24] With this as their starting point, Black theologians like Itumeleng Mosala and Takatso Mofokeng go on to focus on the kinds of scholarly strategies and reading resources that are most appropriate for reading the Bible in the South African context of the 1980s. But a careful reading of their work does provide glimpses of 'other' reading resources and interpretative strategies—the interpretative moves ordinary African 'readers' make.

Drawing from and elaborating on the work of Mosala, Mofokeng argues that the Bible is both a problem and a solution. The 'external' problem of the Bible is the oppressive and reactionary use of the Bible by white Christians. The internal problem is the Bible itself. Like Mosala, he is critical of those who concentrate on only the external problem, those who 'accuse oppressor-preachers of *misusing* the Bible for their oppressive purposes and objectives', or who accuse 'preachers and racist whites of not practising what they preach'. It is clear, Mofokeng argues, that these responses are 'based on the assumption that the Bible is essentially a book of liberation'. While Mofokeng concedes that these responses have a certain amount of truth to them, the crucial point he wants to make is that there are numerous 'texts, stories and traditions in the Bible which lend themselves to only oppressive interpretations and oppressive uses because of their inherent oppressive nature'. What is more, any attempt 'to "save" or "co-opt" these oppressive texts for the oppressed only serve the interests of the oppressors'.[25]

Young blacks in particular, Mofokeng goes on to argue, 'have categorically identified the Bible as an oppressive document by its very nature and to its very core' and suggest that the best option 'is to disavow the Christian faith and consequently be rid of the obnoxious Bible'.[26] Indeed, some 'have zealously campaigned for its expulsion from the oppressed Black community', but, henotes, with little success. The reason for this lack of success, Mofokeng suggests, is

24. Mofokeng, 'Black Christians', p. 34.
25. Mofokeng, 'Black Christians', pp. 37-38.
26. See also Lekoapa P. Masipa, 'The Use of the Bible in Black Theology with Reference to the Exodus Story' (MTh. Thesis, University of Natal, 1997).

largely due to the fact that no easily accessible ideological silo or
storeroom is being offered to the social classes of our people that
are desperately in need of liberation. African traditional religions
are too far behind most blacks while Marxism, is to my mind, far
ahead of many blacks, especially adult people. In the absence of a
better storeroom of ideological and spiritual food, the Christian
religion and the Bible will continue for an undeterminable period
of time to be the haven of the Black masses par excellence.[27]

Given this situation of very limited ideological options, Mofokeng continues, 'Black theologians who are committed to the
struggle for liberation and are organically connected to the struggling Christian people, have chosen to honestly do their best to
shape the Bible into a formidable weapon in the hands of the
oppressed instead of leaving it to confuse, frustrate or even destroy our people'.[28]

But it was not only Black theologians who were shaping the
Bible into a formidable weapon. Mofokeng himself offers us a
glimpse of the 'shaping' work of ordinary 'others' as he characterizes the 'reading' strategies and resources of ordinary black
Christians.

As members of a people whose story of pain, fears and hopes has
been suppressed, they are enabled, by their physical and psycho-
logical scars, together with the analytical tools they have chosen, to
discover the suppressed and forgotten stories of the weak and the
poor of the Bible. These seem, according to them, to be the stories
wherein God is identifying with the forgotten and the weak and is
actively retrieving them from the margins of the social world. It is
through these stories that God the creator of humans is manifested
as the God of the oppressed and accepted as such. This creator
God acts incarnately in Jesus to end the rampant enmity in creation and restore real humanity to people. Only the reading of
these stories of the downtrodden God among the downtrodden of
this world strengthens the tormented faith of the oppressed of our
time, as well as enhancing the quality of their commitment to the
physical struggle for liberation. This discovery constitutes the liberation of the Bible from the clutches of the dominant in the Christian fold who impose the stories that justify their victories onto the
oppressed.[29]

27. Mofokeng, 'Black Christians', p. 40.
28. Mofokeng, 'Black Christians', p. 40.
29. Mofokeng, 'Black Christians', p. 41.

This paragraph of Mofokeng's resonates with the work of Wimbush cited earlier, but Mofokeng is less precise in his description and analysis of 'the analytical tools they [ordinary black South Africans] have chosen'. Like Mosala, Mofokeng is clear that black experience, or the experience of 'blackness',[30] is the starting point of black Bible reading, and like Mosala, he wants to insist, at times, that certain interpretative tools are more appropriate than others. However, and this is my point, there are moments when Mofokeng acknowledges the presence of other reading resources besides those of the black biblical scholar and when he allows for whatever analytical tools ordinary African Christians choose for the interpretative task.

Mosala is more definite, and wants to insist on particular interpretative tools being more appropriate than others. In fact, the central thrust of all his work is to argue that the only appropriate analytical and interpretative tools are historical-materialist ones. But while Mosala does seem to insist that these are the only appropriate interpretative and analytical procedures to be used in the encounter with the Bible, there are moments when even he alludes to other resources in the black community. He argues, for example, that the uncritical 'Word of God' approach of many Black theologians to the Bible has been 'surpassed by the largely illiterate black working class and poor peasantry who have defied the canon of Scripture, with its ruling class ideological basis, by appropriating the Bible *in their own way* using the cultural tools emerging out of their struggle for survival'.[31] Such statements, and the similar sentiments of Mofokeng, require more careful scrutiny. However, because neither Mosala nor Mofokeng elaborate on these strands of their respective analyses, we will have to look elsewhere.

What are the tools that ordinary African interpreters of the Bible use to appropriate the Bible? How do they 'read'? In describing four cases of ordinary indigenous 'readers' reading the

30. Frostin, *Liberation Theology in Tanzania*, pp. 86-87.

31. Itumeleng J. Mosala, 'The Use of the Bible in Black Theology', in Itumeleng J. Mosala and Bhuti Tlhagale (eds.), *The Unquestionable Right to Be Free* (Johannesburg: Skotaville, 1986), pp. 175-99 (184), my emphasis. Unfortunately, Mosala does not elaborate on this.

Bible,[32] I have demonstrated that while there may appear to be some affinities between the reading strategies and resources of ordinary 'readers' and the modes of reading of socially engaged biblical scholars, the situation is more complex. There are certainly interesting similarities, but we must recognize that something fundamentally different is going on in the reading processes of ordinary indigenous 'readers'. As I have indicated, Wimbush suggests that such a hermeneutic is 'characterized by a looseness, even playfulness, vis-à-vis the biblical texts themselves'.[33]

While there are similarities between the reading strategies and resources of what I have called 'ordinary "readers" of the Bible', there are also significant differences. Ordinary 'readers' 'read' the Bible pre-critically. My use of 'pre-critical' is not perjorative; ordinary 'readers' have little option in being so characterized because of the specific technical sense in which I am using the term. They read pre-critically because they have not been trained in the critical modes of reading that characterize biblical scholarship. There is no mystery here; biblical scholars are trained to ask structured and systematic sets of questions (whether they be historical-critical, socio-historical, literary, structuralist, post-structuralist, canonical, etc.) and ordinary 'readers' have not been so trained. In fact, as I have indicated, many ordinary 'readers' are not actually readers at all; they are illiterate hearers, interpreters and retellers of the Bible. So although there may be important similarities between the modes of reading of ordinary 'readers' and the modes of reading of trained readers, there is nevertheless this crucial difference. This difference is crucial in that it helps explain the usefulness of the reading strategies and resources of biblical scholarship to ordinary 'readers' of the Bible. But once again I must stress that my use of the terms 'critical/pre-critical' carries no sense of 'better/worse'. I am using these terms in a carefully specified technical sense.

In noting this difference I am not denying that ordinary African 'readers' read (or hear) the Bible with a critical consciousness. However, while there is definitely a 'critical consciousness' on the part of some ordinary indigenous 'readers', this is not quite the same as the socio-historical approach advocated by, for example,

---

32. West, *Biblical Hermeneutics*, pp. 174-200.
33. Wimbush, 'The Bible and African Americans', pp. 88-89.

Mosala. Ordinary African 'readers' may, and often do, have a general critical consciousness towards society and texts, but they do not have the historical and sociological tools to be critical of the biblical text in the same way as Mosala. When young black workers in the Young Christian Workers movement (YCW) appropriate the Bible as the story of liberation they are doing so on the basis of selected texts (and not various redactional layers) and of selected historical and sociological information (and not a systematic reconstruction of the social system behind the text).[34] The political-critical consciousness of some ordinary 'readers' may predispose them to a critical approach to the Bible, but as ordinary 'readers' this is not their mode of reading.

Similarly, J. Severino Croatto seems to argue that the poor and oppressed actually read the Bible in the way that his in-front-of-the-text mode of reading articulates.[35] But once again it is important to recognize that while many ordinary 'readers' do read the Bible thematically in its final form as a single canonical text, this is not quite the same as the linguistic-symbolic post-critical canonical approach of Croatto. When ordinary 'readers' read the Bible thematically in its final form they begin with creation (and not exodus) and read selectively (and not along 'a semantic axis'). So while poor and marginalized ordinary indigenous 'readers' may be predisposed to such a post-critical in-front-of-the-text reading of the Bible, their own strategies and resources are different.

These are the differences that worry Mosala. Mosala's concern is that such ways of reading and appropriating the Bible

> cannot be allowed to substitute for a theoretically well-grounded biblical hermeneutics of liberation. The reason for this is that, while texts that are against oppressed people may be co-opted by the interlocutors of the liberation struggle, the fact that these texts have their ideological roots in oppressive practices means that the texts are capable of undergirding the interests of the oppressors even when used by the oppressed. In other words, oppressive texts cannot be totally tamed or subverted into liberating texts.[36]

34. West, *Biblical Hermeneutics*, pp. 188-93.
35. Severino Croatto, *Biblical Hermeneutics*, p. 50.
36. Mosala, *Black Theology*, p. 30. Nothing, Mosala later adds, 'could be more subversive to the struggle for liberation than enlisting the oppressors and exploiters as comrades in arms' (p. 33).

Mosala is worried about two things here. First, he is worried that black biblical hermeneutics might suffer from an 'unstructural understanding of the Bible' and, second, that both as a consequence and as a reason, it might also suffer from an 'unstructural understanding' of the black experience and struggle.[37] Central to Mosala's hermeneutics of liberation is the search for a theoretical perspective that can locate both the Bible and the black experience within appropriate socio-historical contexts.[38] As already mentioned, for Mosala a historical-materialist understanding of struggle provides the tools for reading both black history and culture and the Bible.

Mosala's concerns are clear, but are they the whole story? What if, as the discussion of domination and resistance in Chapter 2 suggests, ordinary indigenous Africans have both a more 'structural' understanding of the Bible and their social context than we recognize? What if they have disguised their actual 'structural' understanding in order to survive? And what if they have achieved this 'structural' understanding using resources of their own? What if ordinary indigenous African 'readers' already have their own resources for critically appropriating the Bible? Surely the presence of such already existing resources would be significant, especially if as we are to use local resources, as for example Tinyiko Maluleke urges us to, in the process of reconstructing our country?[39]—particularly if these resources can be traced back in some form to the reading resources of our African ancestors in their transactions with the Bible.

I am not suggesting that there is no place for organic intellectuals or socially engaged biblical scholars and their critical resources.[40] To the contrary, much of my own work demonstrates

37. Mosala, *Black Theology*, p. 32; the phrase 'unstructural understanding' is taken from the work of Gottwald. See also West, *Biblical Hermeneutics*, pp. 136-46 for further discussion of this phrase.

38. Mosala, *Black Theology*, p. 24.

39. Tinyiko Sam Maluleke, 'Black and African Theologies in the New World Order', *Journal of Theology for Southern Africa* 96 (1996), pp. 3-19 (17).

40. Patricia Hill Collins characterizes organic intellectuals as those who 'depend on common sense and represent the interests of their own group' in contrast to what she calls 'academicians' who are 'trained to represent the interests of groups in power'; Patricia Hill Collins, *Black Feminist Thought:*

the creative and critical possibilities of a sharing of resources between socially engaged biblical scholars and ordinary African 'readers' of the Bible,[41] which I want to take further in this book by probing more carefully just what our place in this process may be. But before we can have any place in the process—before we can enter into a meaningful and empowering alliance with ordinary African 'readers'—we must have acknowledged the resources those 'readers' already have. How can we 'drink from our own wells'[42] when we denigrate them or deny their very existence and rely on imported, bottled water (or worse, Coca Cola)? Perhaps ordinary African 'readers' can help us recover readings of the Bible that our training blinds us to; perhaps, to return to an earlier example, ordinary African 'readers' do have resources which tame and subvert what may have been originally oppressive texts.[43] Whatever their 'original' intention—and we must not forget that the notion of 'intention' is itself contested—there are a host of strategies for reading texts against any alleged intention. Critical readers of the Bible have resources for doing this (for example, deconstruction), and, I am arguing, so do ordinary 'readers'—however, we are not as adept at describing their resources as we are at describing (and inscribing) our own.

Wimbush describes the interpretative strategies of African slaves as 'characterized by a looseness, even playfulness' with respect to biblical texts. This description does not seem to suggest the type of 'Word of God' hermeneutics Black and African theologians are charged with by Mosala, Mofokeng and, more recently, Maluleke.[44] I do not want to dwell on or develop this line of argument, but I do want to insist that more careful analysis is required of exactly what particular Black and African theologians mean by their uses of the phrase 'Word of God'.[45] My main point

Knowledge, Consciousness, and the Politics of Empowerment (London: Harper-Collins, 1990), p. 18 n. 5.

41. West, 'And the Dumb Do Speak'.

42. Maluleke, 'Black and African Theologies', p. 3.

43. Deciding whether a text was 'originally' oppressive is not a certain science; see, for example, my discussion of Mosala's and Gunther Wittenberg's respective readings of the Cain and Abel story in West, *Biblical Hermeneutics*, p. 78.

44. Maluleke, 'Black and African Theologies', p. 3.

45. Some analysis of the different ways in which Mosala and Allan Boesak

in this chapter is to give substance to the claim, made in passing, of both Mosala and Mofokeng that ordinary Africans have their own resources for appropriating the Bible for their own purposes, including survival, resistance, liberation and life. As already indicated, Wimbush's work goes some way to supporting such a claim. While Wimbush has attempted to elaborate and support this claim, our problem in South Africa is that we socially engaged biblical scholars (and theologians) have not concentrated on the reading resources and strategies of ordinary African 'readers' of the Bible, but have tended to analyse the methods and approaches of academically trained readers of the Bible. So when we discover that the interpretative tools and procedures of Black and African theologians resemble the Western reading resources of the missionaries and colonialists we should not be surprised—they have mastered their masters' training!

This does not mean, however, that academically trained biblical scholars and theologians are not able to turn their training against the agendas and ideologies of those who trained them. Mosala is an excellent example of a black biblical scholar who has used Western tools to dismantle dominant ideologies. Western modes of reading are not innocent, but neither are those who take them up as weapons of resistance, survival, liberation and life! The Bible is not innocent,[46] but neither are those untrained ordinary African interpreters who have appropriated it. As we will see, not only have they wrested ways of reading from their missionary and colonial masters and madams, but through their experiences they have also found and forged their own ways of 'reading' the Bible in order to fuel the working theologies they live by.

So before we re-envisage the role of the socially engaged biblical scholar in the next chapter, I want to develop in more depth the claim that ordinary Africans have 'reading' resources of their own,

use this phrase can be found in Frostin, *Liberation Theology in Tanzania*, pp. 160-65 and West, *Biblical Hermeneutics*, pp. 122-24.

46. Any claim that the Bible is a Western text is, of course, nonsense. Western imperial forces may have brought this book to most of Africa, but its origins lie elsewhere (including Africa); see Schaaf, *On their Way Rejoicing*. See Tracy, *Plurality and Ambiguity*, for a discussion of the fall from innocence of classic texts, including the Bible.

by characterizing a cluster of interpretative strategies used by ordinary African 'readers'. My account is preliminary, but I hope it will contribute to the further work that needs to be done in this area. Throughout the book I have placed the term 'reading' in inverted commas. This acknowledges that I am using the term both literally, to include literate African readers, and metaphorically, to include illiterate or partially literate African 'readers'. In most of the communities I work with the majority of Bible interpreters are either partially literate or illiterate; and yet they hear, remember and retell the Bible. What they hear, remember and retell is, I want to suggest, a remaking or a 're-membering' of the Bible.

They 'read' differently; their 'reading', I would suggest, is more akin to 'rewriting' than to reading in any scholarly sense. Responding to the damage done by the Bible in Africa, the Zimbabwean theologian Canaan S. Banana called for the rewriting of the Bible.[47] Once again, as both Mosala and Mofokeng note, ordinary Africans are ahead of their trained compatriots. While they do not rewrite the Bible they do 're-member' it. Ordinary African interpreters of the Bible are not as transfixed and fixated by the text as their textually trained pastors and theologians; in Wimbush's words, their hermeneutics is characterized by 'a looseness, even playfulness' towards the biblical text. If they do speak of the Bible as 'Word of God', they do so in senses that are more metaphorical than literal; 'the Book' is more of a symbol than a text.[48] The Bible they work with is always an already 're-membered' 'text'—a text, both written and oral, that has been dismembered, taken apart, and then remade and re-membered.

47. Canaan S. Banana, 'The Case for a New Bible', in Isabel Mukonyora, James L. Cox and Frans J. Verstaelen (eds.), *'Rewriting' the Bible: The Real Issues: Perspectives from within Biblical and Religious Studies in Zimbabwe* (Gweru: Mambo Press, 1993), pp. 17-32.

48. In much of Africa and among Africans in the diaspora the Bible is often used as 'a religio-magical instrument'; see Ndungu, 'The Bible in an African Independent Church', pp. 62-63; Justin Ukpong, 'Port Harcourt Report of the Bible in Africa Project's Findings' (Port Harcourt: Unpublished Report, 1994); and Gosnell L.O.R. Yorke, 'The Bible in the Black Diaspora', in Hannah W. Kinoti and John M. Waliggo (eds.), *The Bible in African Christianity* (Nairobi: Acton Publishers, 1997), pp. 149-52.

I use the term 're-membering', obviously, because of its deriva-
tion from the more familiar 'remembering'. In the South African
context ordinary African interpreters work with a remembered as
well as a read Bible. As Mosala reminds us, ordinary Africans,
particularly in the African Independent Churches, 'have an oral
knowlege of the Bible'. 'Most of their information about the Bible
comes from socialization in the churches themselves as they listen
to prayers and sermons'.[49] The 're-membering' of the Bible is,
therefore, a communal process. Hearing, remembering and
retelling are community acts.[50] This does not imply the absence of
the Bible as text, for although the Bible as text is not central to
the corporate practice of 're-membering', it does have a presence.
Even those who are illiterate have considerable exposure to biblical texts being read. Reflecting on the Kenyan context Nahashon
Ndungu notes 'even the illiterate members [of the Akurinu African Independent Church] take pains to master some verses which
they readily quote when they give their testimonies'.[51] These same
members often carry copies of the Bible so that '[i]f need arises
they can always request a literate member to read for them'.[52] The
remembered Bible and the read Bible reside side by side. Both
have a part in the process of 're-membering'; 're-membering' is
not simply an oral activity.

Translation of the Bible into local languages has, of course,
played a role in removing the remembered and written Bible from
the control of the missionaries and colonialists. Kwame Bediako
goes so far as to say that 'to the credit of the modern missionary
enterprise, the more recent missionary history of Africa…can

49. Itumeleng J. Mosala, 'Race, Classs, and Gender as Hermeneutical
Factors in the African Independent Churches' Appropriation of the Bible',
Semeia 73 (1996), pp. 43-57. Although Mosala's assessment here is based on
African Independent Churches, it applies as well to the so-called main-line
churches; see Jonathan A. Draper, 'Confessional Western Text-Centred
Biblical Interpretation and an Oral or Residual-Oral Context', *Semeia* 73
(1996), pp. 59-77.

50. See Zablon Nthamburi and Douglas Waruta, 'Biblical Hermeneutics
in African Instituted Churches', in Hannah W. Kinoti and John M. Waliggo
(eds.), *The Bible in African Christianity* (Nairobi: Acton Publishers, 1997), pp.
40-57 (52).

51. Ndungu, 'The Bible in an African Independent Church', p. 62.

52. Ndungu, 'The Bible in an African Independent Church', p. 62.

justly be regarded as the history of Bible translation'.[53] Drawing on and developing the work of David B. Barrett, Kenneth Cragg, Philip Stine, Ype Schaaf and especially Lamin Sanneh,[54] Bediako argues that when missionaries or mission societies made the Bible available to an African people in that people's own language, their grip on the gospel was loosened and so too their proprietary claim on Christianity. Translation enabled the Bible to become 'an independent yardstick by which to test, and sometimes to reject, what Western missionaries taught and practised' and in so doing 'provided the basis for developing new, indigenous forms of Christianity'.[55]

The full weight of Bediako's argument, and here he leans heavily on Sanneh's work, is found in the final phase of the argument where it is claimed that in the vernacular Bible Africans were able to discover 'that the God of the Bible had preceded the missionary into the receptor-culture' and that 'Christianity had, in fact, been adequately anticipated'.[56] Translation in this sense is much more than a technical discipline,[57] it is a metaphor for forms of inculturation.

53. Kwame Bediako, 'Epilogue', in Ype Schaaf, *On their Way Rejoicing: The History and Role of the Bible in Africa* (Carlisle: Paternoster Press, 1994), pp. 241-54 (246).

54. David B. Barrett, *Schism and Renewal in Africa: An Analysis of Six Thousand Contemporary Religious Movements* (Nairobi: Oxford University Press, 1968); Kenneth Cragg, *Christianity in World Perspective* (London: Lutterworth Press, 1968); Philip Stine (ed.), *Bible Translation and the Spread of the Church: The Last 200 Years* (Leiden: E.J. Brill, 1990); Lamin Sanneh, *Translating the Message: The Missionary Impact on Culture* (Maryknoll, NY: Orbis Books, 1989).

55. Bediako, 'Epilogue', p. 246. See also Kofi Appiah-Kubi, 'Indigenous African Christian Churches: Sins of Authenticity', in Kofi Appiah-Kubi and Sergio Torres (eds.), *African Theology en Route: Papers from the Pan-African Conference of Third World Theologians, Accra, December 17–23, 1977* (Maryknoll, NY: Orbis Books, 1977), pp. 117-25 (119), and John S. Mbiti, 'The Biblical Basis for Present Trends in African Theology', in Appiah-Kubi and Torres (eds.), *African Theology en Route*, pp. 83-94 (90-91).

56. Kwame Bediako, 'Translatability: Reading the Christian Scriptures in African Languages' (unpublished paper), pp. 1-2.

57. See Sanneh, *Translating the Message*, p. 3.

Whatever we might think of these claims, and there is something both wonderfully subversive and yet uncomfortably conser-
vative about them,[58] we can accept that vernacular translation
hands over the Bible, to some extent, to the ordinary African
'reader'.[59] Translation, then, has a part in the 're-membering' of
the Bible, and the forms of 're-membering' it makes possible can
be investigated. For example, what forms of 'Christianity' emerge
in a context where the first texts translated into the local languages are Genesis and then Luke? Such was the case in the
coastal villages of East Africa among the freed slaves during the
period 1840–70. My question is given additional force because, as
Schaaf notes, these Christians 'became the African pioneers of the
missions who early in the twentieth century would spread the
gospel among the peoples of East Africa'.[60] If both Bediako and
Wimbush are right in their respective arguments—that translation
into the vernacular loosens the control of the missionary on the
message and that the hermeneutic strategies that local communities adopt in order to appropriate the text for themselves are
foundational for subsequent interpretative practice—then more
careful analysis of such transactions would be extremely valuable
in understanding the dynamics and products of 're-membering'.

I also use the term 're-membering' in Wimbush's way, mentioned earlier, to refer to 'a looseness, even a playfulness' towards
the text where interpretation is not controlled by the literal words
of the texts, but by social experience; where texts are heard and
retold more than read; where texts are engaged as stories that
seize and free the imagination; where biblical texts are usually
interpreted collectively; where biblical stories function sometimes
as allegory, as parable or as veiled social criticism in a situation
where survival demands disguised forms of resisting discourse;
where certain texts in the canon are read and others ignored.

Another way of characterizing reading as 're-membering' can
be found in Osayande Obery Hendricks's concept of 'guerrilla
exegesis'.[61] Guerilla exegesis, like 're-membering', takes whatever

58. See Maluleke, 'Black and African Theologies'.

59. Sanneh, *Translating the Message*, pp. 3-5. See also Maluleke, 'Black and
African Theologies', p. 4, and Bediako, 'Epilogue'.

60. Schaaf, *On their Way Rejoicing*, pp. 66-67.

61. Hendricks, 'Guerilla Exegesis'. In what follows I have picked out those

tools and resources are at hand, wherever they may come from, whether indigenous or imported, and uses them to sabotage and subvert dominant readings, to make new things out of old things, to find new truths in unexpected and familiar places, to redefine reality, to empower and inspire. 'Re-membering', like guerilla exegesis, is eclectic and transgressive. 'Re-membering' is bricolage, is improvisation, is jazz. 'Re-membering' is '[u]sing whatever means you have in hand to free the meanings struggling to be freed, even if those means reside outside the bounds of methodological conventionality, outside the bounds of the hegemonic OK'.[62]

Reminding us that 're-membering' is, as Hendricks asserts, 'irreverent', both from a scholarly and an ecclesiastical point of view, Nancy Cardoso Pereira speaks of the necessity of a hermeneutics of smell! Women in Latin America, she argues, can no longer restrict their reading resources to those of tradition or of science, 'but abandoning our trust in them both, we allow our sense of smell to point us to the possibilities of discovering the memory of God's people'. While some traditional and some scientific tools may be of use, 'we do not cease to sniff at the text, to suspect it, even to reject it if it has a bad odour about it'. Women, she claims, 're-create the text, not in itself, but in telling it we re-invent it beginning with ourselves, since we are the owners of our own noses!'[63] 'Re-membering' is olfactory, is reading with the nose, is leading the Bible by the nose!

Finally, what I refer to as 're-membering' can also be characterized in a fifth way. Drawing on the work of Jacques Derrida and Laura Donaldson, Mary McClintock Fulkerson uses the phrase 'engraf(ph)ting' to speak of the reader's 'writing' of the text.

> The Derridean play on the term *graf(ph)t* (combining *graphion*, Greek for stylus, and *graft*, a horticultural practice) evokes the materiality of writing by means of the horticultural practice that joins a cutting of a plant with another rooted one. A graft is other than

characteristics of 'guerilla exegesis' that resonate with my understanding of 're-membering'.

62. Hendricks, 'Guerilla Exegesis', p. 79.

63. Cited in Rosangela Soares De Oliveira, 'Feminist Theology in Brazil', in Ofelia Ortega (ed.), *Women's Vision: Theological Reflection, Celebration, Action* (Geneva: World Council of Churches, 1995), pp. 65-76 (69-70).

the plant, even as it redirects the flow of sap, and depends for its life on the host; it creates a new plant. Similarly, a reading is an engraf(ph)ting on a text; it is not a mirror of a text, a repetition or imitation. A reading writes a text anew, stimulates its flow of meaning in new directions.[64]

The usefulness of this trope 'is the inseparable—indeed, the constitutive—effect of social relations on the writing (production) of reader-practitioners, and the effect of reader-practitioners on the "text" produced'.

> A reading is a graf(ph)ted subject position, a textual position constructed out of the codes of the social formation. In the rewriting of the text, the redirected flow of that text is a splicing that directs our attention to the material relations that bring it into being. The graf(ph)t creates breaks, factures, and joints that mark off the needs, desires, pleasures, and fears of a subject position and elicit previously nonexistent possibilities in the text.[65]

'Re-membering', then, is also 'engraf(ph)ting', particularly if we add to this latter term the South African English sense of 'graft' as 'hard work'[66] and another sense of 'graft', which echoes Scott's account of the hidden transcript, as 'illicit spoils'. 'Re-membering' is a rewriting, a redirecting of meaning. 'Re-membering' writes a text anew from and for a particular social location. 'Re-membering' is hard work, is struggle. 'Re-membering' is forging meaning offstage, often at night.

Because the Bible as book—as text—is always present, even when it is not being read, the potential for the Bible as allegedly determinate text[67] to overwrite what has been 're-membered' is always a possibility. Perhaps this is what Mosala means when he warns that 'oppressive texts cannot be totally tamed or subverted into liberating texts'. His use of the qualifier 'totally' implies that he recognizes that texts can be partially subverted and tamed, but that the text (and its allegedly original intention) can always reassert itself. While text may be less malleable than memory, we

64. Mary McClintock Fulkerson, *Changing the Subject: Women's Discourses and Feminist Theology* (Minneapolis: Fortress Press, 1994), p. 152.

65. Fulkerson, *Changing the Subject*, pp. 152-53.

66. This usage is also listed in *The Oxford English Dictionary* (1989) as slang.

67. See Fulkerson, *Changing the Subject*, for a detailed poststructuralist account of the unstable text and readers as producers of meaning.

must not underestimate the powerful presence of the 're-mem-bered' 'text' as it permeates the life of the community. As with the initial encounter with the Bible, its use by the dominant (whether they read it with or against its alleged original intention) can be countered by the many moves that constitute 're-membering'.[68] This, anyway, is my contention.

A brief example may be useful to illustrate my arguments.[69] The woodcut (see illustration overleaf) by Azaria Mbatha,[70] a South African artist and ordinary African Bible reader, is an example of 're-membering'. For example, Mbatha's interpretation, unlike that of the missionaries and successions of Sunday School teachers and preachers after them, locates the story in Africa, which is where most of the Joseph Story as told in Genesis takes place, and he reads the story from and for his African context. The characters, themes and concerns are African, with the symbols and ideas coming specifically from the Zulu tradition and culture.[71] Mbatha's reading recovers and reclaims some of the 'Africaness' of the Bible, and reminds us that the Bible belongs to Africa as well as the Western world. Mbatha's reading also remembers the pre-colonial past, a past which 'we need to be reminded by and about', and which 'we as Africans were compelled to forget'.[72]

Creative figures in post-colonial contexts, like Mbatha, whether they work with images, mirrors, medicines, or the written word, are 'experimental practitioners' in that they 'try to make universal signs speak to particular realities'; 'their activities are in fact a means of *producing* historical consciousness: they seek to shape

---

68. There is also a deeper issue at stake here; ordinary 'readers' appear to accept poststructuralist notions of 'text' that are only recently being recognized by biblical scholars (see Fulkerson, *Changing the Subject,* and the articles in Capel Anderson and Staley [eds.], *Taking It Personally*).

69. I have discussed this example in more detail elsewhere; see West, 'Difference and Dialogue', and West, 'Re-membering the Bible in South Africa'.

70. The woodcut is used with the permission of the artist.

71. Azaria Mbatha, *Im Herzen des Tigers: In the Heart of the Tiger.* Text by Werner Eichel (Wuppertal: Peter Hammer Verlag, 1986), p. 6.

72. Mbatha, *In the Heart of the Tiger,* p. 7; 'It was European civilization which brought the end of African civilization and replaced it with its own. I cannot find the words to describe what a terrible crime this is' (p. 8).

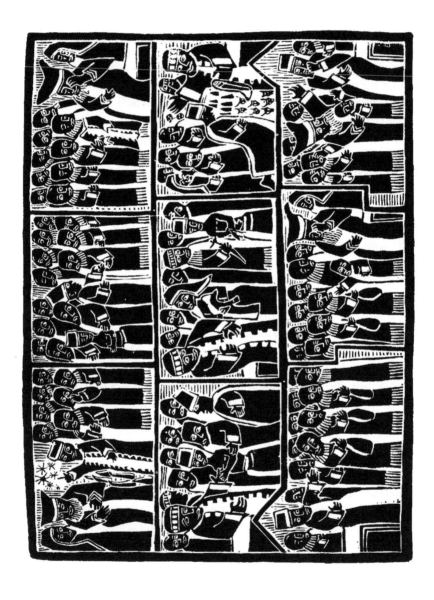

the inchoateness, the murky ambiguity of colonial encounters into techniques of empowerment and signs of collective representation'.[73] This re-making of universal signs in the specifically South African colonial matrix of missionary endeavour and the encroachments of modern capitalism has drawn readers like Mbatha 'into a conversation with the culture of modern capitalism—only to find themselves enmeshed…in *its* order of signs and values'. And yet, 'even as they are encompassed by the European capitalist system—consumed, ironically as they consume its goods and texts—they often seek to seize its symbols, to question their authority and integrity, and to reconstruct them in their own image'.[74] Mbatha's woodcut, both in its form and in its images, might be interpreted as being engaged in such reconstruction or 're-membering'. The woodcut, an African form, seizes and remakes the left-to-right and top-to-bottom conventions of colonial text to tell an African story of struggle from a European brought book—the Bible.[75]

Clearly Mbatha's 're-membering' of the Joseph Story is a resisting 're-membering'. Mbatha's woodcut portrays the perspective of Africa in its concern for the community and in its concentration on human oppression. Every panel of the woodcut is filled with characters. This is not a story of an individual but the story of a clan and of a community. It is a story of *ubuntu*: a person is a person because of other people. But it is also a story of powerlessness and isolation.[76] The threat to *ubuntu* is recognized in panels 2, 4, 7 and 8 where Mbatha's interpretation 'from below' focuses on the human being as object. In each of these panels a human being is being exchanged for money; the human being is an object to be bought and sold. Panels 2 and 4 depict the two times Joseph is sold: to Ishmaelite/Midianite traders by his brothers and by the Ishmaelites/Midianites to an Egyptian officer of Pharaoh. In panel 7, Joseph, who is now an important and powerful official in Egypt and who has not yet been recognized by his brothers, forces the brothers to leave Simeon behind as a hostage

---

73. Comaroff and Comaroff, *Of Revelation and Revolution*, p. xxii.
74. Comaroff and Comaroff, *Of Revelation and Revolution*, p. xii.
75. Panels are numbered from left to right, and read from top to bottom.
76. Mbatha, *In the Heart of the Tiger*, pp. 7-9.

so that they will return to Joseph with Benjamin.[77] And as panel 8 indicates, Jacob is forced to send Benjamin as a ransom for Simeon and in exchange for food. Mbatha recognizes, and reminds us of, the suffering of those who are manipulated and exploited by the powerful.

Mbatha's reading also probes the presence of the powerful, those 'who live in this world at the expense of the weak'.[78] The pain of their presence in the Joseph Story is amplified by his recognition that the oppression of the weak is perpetrated and perpetuated not only by those outside the community (panels 4 and 5), but also by members of the community (panels 1, 2, 3, 7 and 8). This is genuinely terrible: the recognition that the ability and will to dominate and destroy lies among us in the family and community.[79] *Ubuntu* is broken, families are separated and communities moved, not only by forces without but also by forces within.

By foregrounding the youngest sons, Joseph and Benjamin, Mbatha recovers the African (and the story's) emphasis on community continuity. 'When a child is born the chain of ancestors grows by another link',[80] hence the isolation, alienation, fear, and hopelessness of Jacob and Leah (or Rachel, or Bilhah, or Zilpah)[81] in panels 1, 3 and 8. Not only is the continuity of community threatened, but a connecting link with the *amadlozi* (ancestors) is also lost,[82] because the *amadlozi* often speak through young children in dreams and visions (panel 1).[83] Furthermore,

77. Some of the Bible studies on which my comments are based took place at the time when Nelson Mandela and others from the liberation movements were being released from prison, and there was much discussion about whether these leaders, once they held political office, would use their power to empower others or to dominate.

78. Mbatha, *In the Heart of the Tiger*, p. 5.

79. Mbatha, *In the Heart of the Tiger*, p. 10.

80. Mbatha, *In the Heart of the Tiger*, p. 21.

81. I discuss the women in the Joseph Story in more detail in West, 'Difference and Dialogue'.

82. Mbatha, *In the Heart of the Tiger*, p. 41.

83. I wish to acknowledge the assistance of two colleagues, Dumisani Phungula and Bafana Khumalo, in helping me to explore this point. This is also an appropriate place to acknowledge all the ordinary indigenous African readers whose readings I am re-presenting.

a child who dies lacks the wisdom and experience of the community to become a significant ancestor who will guarantee continuity between the past and the future.[84]

My final illustration from Mbatha's 're-membering' reading of the Joseph Story has to do with his ending. Mbatha ends with *ubuntu* being restored (panel 9); the family is together again, and the tears are tears of joy, not pain. This is an empowering and enabling ending for people in Africa, proclaiming as it does that forces of colonialization and conquest will not have the final say. However, the actual textual ending of the Joseph Story is more ambiguous. Does the story end here or does it end with Joseph expropriating the land and enslaving the people (Gen. 47.13-25)? Scholars are not in agreement; the final chapters of Genesis contain an array of fragmentary texts. There are a number of possible endings to the Joseph Story. And this brings me to the primary point of this illustration: Mbatha's 're-membering' does interpret the Joseph Story quite differently from the missionaries from whom he first heard it, but he does not do so in a way that dismisses the text. The biblical text remains, but it is 're-membered'.

Earlier in this chapter I used the word 'transaction' to refer to the encounter of indigenous Africans with the Bible. I have used this word, with its economic and legal connotations, to signify that this process is not innocent. When the Bible was brought to Africa it was part of 'a package deal'. However, the missionaries and colonialists did not always have their own way; ordinary Africans have wrested the Bible from their grip. As Maluleke reminds us, 'While oppression and imperialism have been real and ruthless, Africans have at a deeper level negotiated and survived the scourge—by relativizing it, resisting it, and modifying it with uncanny creativity'.[85] In this chapter I am making the same point about the Bible. While the Bible has been used for purposes of oppression and imperialism, both because of the ideologies of those who have used it and because of the ideologies intrinsic to it, ordinary Africans have at a deeper, often hidden, level negotiated and transacted with the Bible and partially appropriated the Bible—by

---

84. Mbatha, *In the Heart of the Tiger*, p. 25.
85. Maluleke, 'Black and African Theologies', p. 8.

relativizing it, resisting it, and modifying it with uncanny creativity. This is what Wimbush means by 'a looseness, even playfulness' towards the text and what I mean by 're-membering'.

Although I have argued that we must be more careful, precise, and analytical in our use of terms like 'Word of God', whether we use the term ourselves or whether we use it to refer to the hermeneutical approaches of others, I agree with Maluleke when he says that while many African Christians 'may mouth the Bible-is-equal-to-the-Word-of-God formula, they are actually creatively pragmatic and selective in their use of the Bible so that the Bible may enhance rather than frustrate their life struggles'.[86] Ordinary African 'readers' do not 'read' as we do. Biblical scholars and theologians, even socially engaged biblical scholars and theologians, may not approve of the ways in which ordinary Africans work with the Bible. They may not like the manner in which ordinary African 'readers' remake and 're-member' the resources that they have taken from biblical scholars. But, I would argue, we cannot ignore the interpretative resources of ordinary African 'readers'.

As I will elaborate in the next chapter, I am not calling for a romanticizing or uncritical acceptance of these resources; rather, my argument and appeal are that we must recognize and understand the resources ordinary African 'readers' use in their encounters with the Bible. In so doing we may learn something, both about the Bible, our interpretative methods, and ourselves—if we are willing to participate with them (bringing our own reading resources) in their 're-membering'. I would go further; unless we are willing to participate in the reading process 'with' ordinary Africans we will lack the necessary local resources for recovering and rebuilding what the missionaries, colonialists, and apartheid have dismembered; we will also be better prepared to resist the insidious and invidious advance of globalization in all its various forms.

So the reminder remains. By arguing that we might have resources to offer to ordinary readers of the Bible I do not mean us to forget that they have resources of their own with which to read with us. They too offer us other ways to read. The contextual Bible study process is, as we will see in the next chapter, a locale where the socially engaged biblical scholar and ordinary reader

---

86. Maluleke, 'Black and African Theologies', p. 13.

of the Bible share their resources, where subjugated and incipient readings and theologies may begin to emerge and may perhaps be openly declared, where we can recognize whether our 'working' readings and theologies resonate with those of others we live and work with, and where we together give shape to counterideologies—resisting readings and theologies that bring survival, liberation, and life. There is a place here for the socially engaged biblical scholar, although it is not perhaps the prominent place we expected.

5 |

Knowing our Place

Given my analysis, what is our place in the 'reading' process? Contextual Bible study work in South Africa has begun to recognize that something like Scott's analysis is a more adequate and accurate understanding of our experience. Resisting and potentially liberating and transforming readings (and theologies) are already present *in some form* in communities of the poor and marginalized. I emphasize the phrase 'in some form' to remind us of the important insight that both Scott and the Comaroffs offer us in their respective analyses of domination and resistance, namely, that the range of forms of the discourse of the dominated is great, including speech acts, gestures, performances, rituals, and many other practices, and that the dimensions of discourse extend from the incipient and inchoate to the explicit and articulate. Where the discourse is explicit and articulate the intellectual seems to have little role to play; however, where the discourse is incipient and inchoate, the contribution of the socially engaged biblical scholar and the contextual Bible study process may be substantial. It would seem that in such cases the contextual Bible study provides processes, critical resources, and a safe social site in which the unarticulated (and primarily religious) responses to domination of individuals are given expression in language, symbol and ritual, and, if they carry effective meaning for the group, become the social property of the group.

Several points must be kept in view by way of explanation. By insisting that contextual Bible study begins with the reality of the *organized* poor and marginalized, socially engaged biblical scholars always find themselves working with groups who are internally structured and who have a clear sense of identity. The Institute for the Study of the Bible (ISB), a project in which poor and marginalized readers of the Bible and socially engaged biblical scholars collaborate, adopts this position in order to recognize and equalize the power relations implicit in the interface between socially engaged biblical scholars and ordinary 'readers' of the Bible. So we only work with groups that can 'talk back'. Sometimes the invitation to the ISB comes from already organized groups, but there are often times when we are approached by one or two individuals; in such cases we ask them to mobilize others and to organize themselves into a group before we accept their invitation to come into their community. The groups we work with, whether they have a long history of meeting together or have been more recently constituted, share two important characteristics. First, they are formed by members of a particular community who share similar experiences of domination, and second, they have found a safe sequestered social site where the control, surveillance and repression of the dominant, whoever they may be in a particular context, are least able to reach. The second condition is what allows members of the group to talk freely at all, while the first ensures that they have something to talk about.[1]

By only working with organized groups—groups that have secured social space and set up structures and group processes that maintain the space and sustain group dynamics—contextual Bible study can be said to provide both a place and the processes in which an offstage subculture can articulate a counterideology. For each subaltern, to use Spivak's term, who knows more or less what attitudes and values lie behind her 'working' readings and theology and, if less reliably, what lies behind those of other subalterns in her group,[2] contextual Bible study provides both a place and the democratic group processes for discerning whether her 'working' readings and theology resonate with and are representative of the group.

The dynamics of articulating, discerning and owning what is incipient and inchoate deserve careful description and analysis in each particular context in which they occur, so all I can do here is to present the parameters within which specific manifestations operate. The hidden transcript, as Scott reminds us, is never a language apart. It is in constant argument with dominant discourses,[3] continually demanding some form of response to

1. See Scott, *Domination*, p. 120.
2. Scott, *Domination*, p. 67.
3. Scott, *Domination*, p. 135.

material exploitation, colonialism, sexism and racism, even if this response must often take a disguised form. But because the argument demands a presence in the public transcript it must of necessity often use the resources of the dominant ideology that prevails in the public transcript; however, as I have already indicated, in the artful hands of the dominated the dominant discourse 'is capable of carrying an enormous variety of meanings, including those that are subversive of their use as intended by the dominant'.[4] This explains why in contextual Bible study initial responses of participants to themes and texts may appear to conform to the public transcript. Participants are testing the waters to see if it is really safe to venture any deeper. As trust and a sense of security grows a more nuanced listening usually discloses a more ambiguous and polysemic expression that is capable of two readings, one which is innocuous, so providing an avenue of retreat if challenged, and one which is subversive, 'smuggling…portions of the hidden transcript, suitably veiled, onto the public stage'.[5]

Because the social locations in which subordinate groups can speak with real safety are fairly restricted, the effective social reach of a particular hidden transcript may be quite limited and may not extend beyond a particular social and/or geographical sector of the community. So, for example, African women in one part of an informal settlement may have little opportunity to speak with women in another part. However, to the degree that the conditions of subordination for women are relatively uniform across, for example, the informal settlement, we would expect there to be 'a comparable family resemblance in their hidden transcript'. By bringing women together within such a community, the contextual Bible study process offers a place, an opportunity, and resources for these women to probe the extent to which their (often incipient and inchoate) hidden transcripts overlap and intersect as they read the Bible together. As particular women offer their tentative articulations they are implicitly testing the extent of a particular hidden transcript—the extent to which, metaphorically speaking, those with comparable hidden transcripts in a society form a single power grid. Where there are differences in the hidden transcript, participants will withdraw

---

4. Scott, *Domination*, pp. 102-103.
5. Scott, *Domination*, p. 157.

their readings, recognizing the lack of connection and the 'leaking' of power from their social grid. Where clear resonances or close relatives in the hidden transcript are discerned, participants elaborate and amplify their articulations, drawing power from the social grid; when this happens 'its mobilizing capacity as a symbolic act is potentially awesome', portending a whole range of possibilities.[6]

The *presence* of socially engaged biblical scholars is another element in the process of what is incipient and inchoate being articulated and potentially becoming the social property of the group. There is, it would seem, a role for Gramsci's organic intellectual or Max Weber's 'pariah-intelligentsia'[7]—but a more modest one than we might have initially assumed. Socially engaged biblical scholars (and theologians) can be of use. Not only are they the bearers of additional potentially useful critical resources, to which we will turn shortly, but they usually inhabit the boundary regions which are the site of 'unremitting struggle' between the dominant and the dominated.[8] Boundaries are dangerous, precisely because of their ambiguity,[9] and so are those who cross boundaries. So, it is only the 'called' and 'converted' biblical scholar who may be of service to poor and marginalized communities—those who have betrayed the hidden discourse of the dominant and who have chosen to be partially constituted by the hidden discourse of the dominated.[10]

Boundary crossers not only contribute spatially, helping to chart more clearly where the boundaries are. By offering resources that cross boundaries in and of time, socially engaged biblical scholars are able to open up potential 'lines of connection' between present and past communities of faith.[11] In terms of Scott's analysis of domination and resistance this appears to be a particularly

6. Scott, *Domination*, pp. 223-27.
7. Max Weber, *The Sociology of Religion* (Boston: Beacon Press, 1964).
8. Scott, *Domination*, p. 14.
9. Robert J. Schreiter, *Constructing Local Theologies* (Maryknoll, NY: Orbis Books, 1985), p. 66.
10. I am not sure that intellectuals from without the community ever have access to the hidden transcript; the zone between the hidden and public transcripts, what Scott calls 'infrapolitics' (*Domination*, p. xiii), may be all we ever inhabit.
11. Schreiter, *Local Theologies*, p. 18.

important contribution. The systematic and structured sets of questions that constitute the work of biblical scholars may provide other ways of 're-membering' and so appropriating the biblical text, and in so doing may enable what is incipient to be owned by the reading community. As I have argued, local communities of poor and marginalized believers have their own hermeneutics of resistance and survival with which they 're-member' the Bible and construct their 'working' theologies.[12] They may be naive and pre-critical, unsystematic and scattered, and they may draw incon-gruously on a range of symbols, rituals, readings and ideas, but they are theirs—they are what they live by.[13] In some cases these readings and theologies resonate with the readings and theologies of their churches; but often they do not, and so they have to be disguised and hidden. Often what is proclaimed in the pulpits, what is sung in the hymns and songs, what is listened to in the liturgy, and what is performed in the cultic rituals, only partially resonates with the 'working' readings and theologies of ordinary people. People then, for example, belong to the Anglican church by day and to a Zionist church by night—if they are fortunate enough to find a place to belong to by night where their incipient 'working' theology resonates with the 'official' theology of the church. Yet even here, in this marginal site, there may not be a place for the readings and theologies of some—for example, of women.

When official or received readings are not meaningful, power-ful and true, then ordinary 'readers' only have their own resources for 're-membering' the biblical tradition. For many this may mean a constant sense of discontinuity between their 're-membered' 'working' readings and theologies and the biblical tradition as they have encountered it. However, while working with socially engaged biblical scholars they have access to other resources—re-sources which offer other possibilities for continuity with other parts of the tradition. The interpretative resources of socially engaged biblical scholars offer forms of access to the boundaries

12. The 'working' theologies of ordinary Africans are often what Delores Williams calls 'survival' theologies; see Delores Williams, *Sisters in the Wilder-ness: The Challenge of Womanist God-Talk* (Maryknoll, NY: Orbis Books, 1993), pp. 194-99.

13. See Cochrane, 'Circles of Dignity', pp. 90, 181.

of the biblical tradition that are not available to ordinary 'readers', and in so doing they provide opportunities for lines of connection between the 'working' readings and theologies of poor and marginalized believers and previously inaccessible parts of the biblical tradition. Meyers' reconstructed Eve and Gottwald's reconstructed Moses group offer potential places in which readers can locate themselves; more importantly, the interpretative moves Meyers and Gottwald make extend the range of resources ordinary readers have for making their own connections. Being able to find lines of connection is potentially empowering because, as Rosemary Radford Ruether reminds us, to find glimmers of what is authentic and true for us in 'submerged and alternative traditions' is to 'assure oneself that one is not mad or duped'.[14]

Because Africans were confronted, converted and catechized with particular parts and peculiar interpretations of Bible, it is these that have constituted the raw material of their 're-membering'. Organic intellectuals and other socially engaged biblical scholars and theologians open up additional parts of and perspectives on the Bible. Neglected and forgotten texts become available; those parts of the canon ignored by the missionaries and colonialists are now read; alternative forms of access to the very edges of the tradition are found. A plurality of perspectives open up and offer unexpected places of connection with the biblical tradition. In short, our additional reading strategies and tools provide increased capacities for critical interpretation and appropriation.

Different interpretative interests offer different forms for finding a place in the biblical tradition with which to establish continuity. And while most ordinary 'readers' we have worked with have little problem with acknowledging moments of discontinuity, their search for places of continuity is a more common tendency. Continuity may be with reconstructed sectors and their struggles behind the text, with untold stories, neglected themes and unfamiliar characters in the text, or with potential worlds projected in front of the text which intersect with the experiences 'readers' bring to the reading process. In these and other ways, ordinary poor and marginalized 'readers' can make lines of connection

14. Ruether, *Sexism*, p. 18; West, *Biblical Hermeneutics*, pp. 126-28.

with parts of the tradition not previously encountered, particularly those parts which are not usually resources for dominant readings and theologies.

In those places where socially engaged biblical scholars and poor and marginalized 'readers' of the Bible read together there are indications that the various interpretative interests of socially engaged biblical scholars can provide alternative access to parts of the tradition that may source and resource poor and marginalized communities. Sources for survival, liberation and life in the biblical tradition may be scarce, and we may have to search for them in the cracks, gaps and absences of the forms of the tradition we have received. But, it seems, there are places in which socially engaged biblical scholars and readers of the Bible in poor and marginalized communities can locate lines of connection, where subjugated and incipient readings and theologies can be articulated and owned, where we can discover whether our 'working' readings and theologies resonate with those of others we live and work with, and where we share our resources and give shape to resisting and reconstructing readings and theologies that bring survival, liberation and life.

The readiness, in my experience, with which ordinary African 'readers' have embraced the otherness of our resources demonstrates their openness to critical resources. However, the way in which ordinary African 'readers' have taken up these critical resources demonstrates that they have not abandoned the array of interpretative resources they already possess. On receiving critical resources ordinary African 'readers' do not become purists who pursue particular interpretative perspectives. They do not; they do not because they read for purposes other than the production of academic papers—they 'read' for survival, liberation, and life.[15] Our offerings as socially engaged biblical scholars may make a contribution to their struggle for survival, liberation, and life, but our contributions too will be 're-membered'—whether we approve or not.

Emmanuel Shoroma, a postgraduate student in one of my courses, offers an illuminating example of the importance of locating lines of connection and of the relentless 're-membering' of ordinary 'readers' in a course paper which reflects on a Bible

15. Fulkerson, *Changing the Subject*, pp. 142-47.

study he facilitated, in which he attempted to implement aspects of the contextual Bible study process.[16] A small group of rural African 'readers' who were interested in the issue of worshipping/venerating ancestors (*badimo*) chose Lk. 9.28-36 as the basis for a Bible study. For one of the male readers, Shoroma notes, Moses and Elijah were the ancestors of Jesus and the disciples and this text shows them speaking with Jesus. According to this reader, this text best explains his belief in ancestors, that even though they have died, they are capable of waking up and engaging in a dialogue with those they loved. So, for him, ancestors are alive somewhere, waiting to be consulted. Another reader, this time a woman, responded in support, saying that the presence of Jesus with these Jewish ancestors is proof enough that Jesus also consulted them in his prayers and that they gave him courage to carry on with the work of God. The disciples, she continued, also appreciated it when they saw their ancestors with Jesus and therefore said to him, 'Master, it is good for us to be here'. Yet another reader, a young man, stood up to indicate his agreement with this line of argument. He argued that just as the disciples had wanted to please their ancestors by building them tabernacles, so too ought they to respect their ancestors and sometimes to make them happy by having a feast (*mophaso*) in their honour.

At this point in the discussion Shoroma notes that one of the three trained readers present (perhaps a minister/priest/pastor?) asked the young man what he thought of v. 35, where a voice was heard from the clouds saying, 'This is my beloved son, hear him'. This question was clearly a form of challenge to the point of view being expressed, because the trained reader continued to point out that after the voice of God had spoken, Jesus was found alone, and Moses and Elijah were nowhere to be seen. Before the young man could respond, another of the trained readers stood up to state that he thought that God, by speaking and so overshadowing the images of Elijah and Moses was trying to refocus the faith of the disciples, away from Moses and Elijah, on to Jesus, God's only begotten son.

---

16. In what follows I have tried to maintain something of the flavour of Shoroma's commentary, which is often a literal English translation of the original language in which the Bible study took place.

The ordinary readers would not, however, be silenced, one of them objecting to the term 'images'. He asked whether images can speak, because according to him Moses and Elijah appeared as real people who could even speak to Jesus. They were not mere images. Shoroma then intervened with a lengthy response, arguing that the transfiguration was a kind of vision, given to the disciples by God to blot out their doubts about the messiahship of Jesus. God, it seemed to him, wanted to show that the Law, represented by Moses, and the Prophets, represented by Elijah, were pointing to and found their fulfillment in Jesus Christ, the promised messiah.

Discussion then continued around the question of whether or not they ought to consult and mention ancestors in their praying. Shoroma and his trained colleagues, influenced to some extent by contextual Bible study concerns, did not insist on their interpretation, although they were clearly unhappy with the position of the other, ordinary 'readers'. Having allowed the Bible study to be shaped to a greater extent than was the custom by ordinary rural 'readers', and having adopted other aspects of the contextual Bible study process, Shoroma recognized elements of a 'working' reading emerge as lines of connection were established between their experience and this text. And even when the three trained readers each in turn presented counter lines of connection, the ordinary 'readers' persisted, although in a more ambiguous manner. So one of the final responses Shoroma records in his study is by an ordinary 'reader' who points out that he still encounters some problems with the dominant view, represented by the three trained readers, 'because these dead people appear alive and talking in the passage'. Furthermore, he adds, there are people in his community who confess to having been visited by the dead and instructed by them to do certain things in that village. Thus it is still difficult for him not to believe in the ancestors.

The Bible study ended here. However, Shoroma gave an oppportunity for two closing comments. One of the trained readers volunteered to be the first commentator. He told the group that God reminds us in Exod. 20.1-3 that 'He' [*sic*] is our God and that God does not want us to have other gods. He stated further that the text the group had discussed showed that God would like us to know we need to obey God's son Jesus Christ in our lives.

'He [*sic*] is the only mediator between God and man', he concluded. Then one of the ordinary 'readers' stood up. He said that
he had appreciated the Bible study process and had learned
much from other participants. He said that he 'now sees his way
clearly and will reconsider his position with regard to the theme.
He expressed hope that the Lord will help him make his things
right and wished that it could also be the same with everybody in
the house.' With this he sat down.

This is a fascinating example of the process I have attempted to
explain, and clearly demonstrates both the possibilities and the
pitfalls of 'reading with'. The close and contextual reading process initiated by Shoroma, a trained reader, offered a range of
reading resources and opened up potential lines of connection
between the lived faith of ordinary Africans and the Bible. While
there was space, ordinary readers used these additional critical
resources to articulate their own incipient readings. However, as
the space was shut down—as survelliance and control were exerted—so they retreated, once again, to the type of ambiguous
response evidenced above in the final comment of an ordinary
'reader'.

The eclectic, strategic and ideological moves ordinary 'readers'
make may feel strange to biblical scholars who are more familiar
with a structured and disciplined reading practice. But we must
remember that theirs are readings they live by in a way we do not.
In the apt words of Hendricks, such readings use 'guerilla
exegesis'; they are readings that are '[i]rreverent when it need be,
devotional when it can be'. They are readings '[f]or bricoleurs.
For folk unashamed of popular culture. For folk who can appreciate the unalloyed magnificence of everyday genius'.[17] Also, the
readings ordinary 'readers' generate may pose significant problems for pastors and priests who feel they have to represent
received readings. Shoroma clearly felt uncomfortable with the
use the group was making of his reading resources, and so tried to
reassert control over the process; in this he was only partially successful, as what was incipient and inchoate shouldered its way on
to the stage and only reluctantly left the stage when ordered to do
so.

17. Hendricks, 'Guerilla Exegesis', p. 78.

We may not approve, but at the very least the socially engaged biblical scholar ought to be willing to be made use of.[18] Yet being of use should not be enough; we should want to be partially constituted by 'their' otherness. We too must be willing to read 'other-wise'. I want to make a number of points here. First, with respect to the reading process I have called 're-membering', I doubt that the trained reader can return to this form of reading, and I am not calling for a romantic return to pre-critical modes of reading. My cause is different; I want us socially engaged biblical scholars to see something of ourselves in the other. For example, Daniel Patte does just this when he argues that our critical readings are usually informed by our pre-critical readings.[19] I concur with Patte: there are elements of 're-membering' in our critical readings. Systematic and structured though our interpretative selections and combinations may be, they are not innocent. Even our most rigorously critical readings show glimpses of our social interests and agendas. In other words, my first point is that there is something of the reading practices of 'the other' in ourselves—we too participate in forms of 're-membering', we just hide them with scholarly slight of hand![20] Again, I must stress that I am not asking for a romanticizing or uncritical acceptance of these 'reading' practices; my argument and appeal in this first point is that we must recognize and understand the resources ordinary African 'readers' use in their encounters with the Bible. We must recognize *how* 'they' read. In so doing we may learn something—about the Bible, text, our interpretative methods and ourselves.

Secondly, the sharing of our critical resources—critical in that they ask structured and systematic sets of questions about the Bible—so that they become, potentially, a part of the eclectic and strategic reading practice of others, involves for us an ethic of risk. This 'ethic of risk' requires *both* that I recognize the partiality of

18. Albert Nolan, 'Work, the Bible, Workers, and Theologians: Elements of a Workers' Theology', *Semeia* 73 (1996), pp. 213-20.

19. Daniel Patte, *Ethics of Biblical Interpretation: A Reevaluation* (Louisville, KY: Westminster/John Knox Press, 1995).

20. It can be argued that allowing any role to the reader in the construction of meaning requires some form of 're-membering' (see Fulkerson, *Changing the Subject*, pp. 133-40).

my particular choices *and* that I continue to struggle with particular communities of the poor and oppressed.[21] Like Sharon
Welch whose phrase I have used here, I recognize the risk in the
particularity and partiality of my forms of social engagement; but I
also recognize the risk in the acts of selection and combination I
make when I use critical 'scholarly' resources.

Part of what constitutes my continuity with the biblical tradition
are the resources of biblical scholarship, and so I am accountable
to that community. And although I am also accountable to local
communities of the poor and marginalized, I cannot simply allow
my social agenda to be read into the biblical tradition; the integrity of my own subjectivity would require that I rather abandon
the tradition. So while 'reading with' those who read from the
margins for survival, liberation and life partially constitutes the
choices I make and the person I am becoming, I have to acknowledge some form of accountability to the structured and systematic
(and allegedly non-selective)[22] resources of biblical studies which
have also partially constituted me, and therefore some form of
responsibility in my use of them.[23] But the risk remains in that
I must choose from among (the undeniably indeterminate) resources of biblical scholarship. Because there are no longer
'assured results', only tentative preliminary approximations with
no prospects of convincing solutions,[24] many scholars refuse to
choose.[25] But I must choose, in both selection and combination,
because I am accountable to those who have called me to read the
Bible with them. And when I do choose, my choices are shaped

---

21. Welch, *Communities of Resistance*, p. 26.

22. The concern for critical modes of reading that are non-selective is, as I
have indicated, a central concern of many socially engaged biblical scholars,
who argue that the selective reading practices of the poor and marginalized
are usually turned against them by dominant forces. See West, *Biblical
Hermeneutics*, pp. 131-73 for a detailed discussion of this concern.

23. Hendricks, 'Guerrilla Exegesis', p. 88, calls this being 'solid but subversive scholars'!

24. Francis Watson, *Text, Church and World: Biblical Interpretation in Theological Perspective* (Grand Rapids: Eerdmans, 1994), p. 58.

25. Scholars may also refuse to choose for other reasons, although usually
they do make undeclared, covert, choices.

both by my interpretative and my social interests. So, in this sense too, the risk is one of particularity and partiality.[26]

Our critical ways of working with text do not distance us from such choices; indeed, if it is true, as Daniel Patte asserts, that our 'critical interpretation', and the phrase is his, 'is a praxis that is intrinsically ethical, because from its starting point to its concluding point it is structured by concerns for others (and the Other)',[27] then I must continually choose to embrace the risk that comes with such an ethic, namely, the risk of choosing to be partially constituted by particular communities of the poor and marginalized—those who have most often been the victims of dominant readings of the Bible, those who are most 'other'—even though such a choice is partial.

Thus far I have spoken of an ethic of risk as it pertains to me and other socially engaged biblical scholars. But those we read with risk more than we do when they share with us not only their resources for reading, including whatever ways they have of locating lines of connection with the biblical tradition, but also the 'working' readings (and theologies) their lives depend on. Our risk offers them resources for reading, their risk redeems us.

My third and final point has to do with a more profound sense of 'knowing our place' in the reading process with ordinary African 'readers'. Owning up to who we are, to our social location, is becoming a constitutive element of our reading practice as biblical scholars,[28] but I am not sure that this is enough. As biblical studies begins to absorb (coopt?) reader-orientated literary theory and the cultural studies movement 'it is becoming yet more clear that scholarly discourses themselves have histories and socio-economic locations'.[29] But does acknowledging this, important as it is, require of us nothing more than saying who we are and then carrying on with business as usual? I think not. Socially engaged biblical scholars, and here I am speaking primarily about

---

26. West, 'No Integrity without Contextuality'.

27. Patte, *Ethics of Biblical Interpretation*, p. 2.

28. Patte, *Ethics of Biblical Interpretation*; Segovia and Tolbert (eds.), *Reading from this Place*; and the essays in *Semeia* 72, which explore the role of autobiography in biblical criticism.

29. Mark G. Brett, 'Interpreting Ethnicity', in Mark G. Brett (ed.), *Ethnicity and the Bible* (Leiden: E.J. Brill, 1996), pp. 3-22 (5).

people like myself, ought to allow themselves to be partially constituted by 'their' life struggles—the life struggles of 'the other'.
Our place is not only to offer and receive resources for trans-
formative readings, our place is to be transformed by the 'reading' process. It is not enough to own up to who we are; we must
not be content to remain the same and to continue with business—and I use the word deliberately—as usual. It is not enough
to follow scholarly fashion by having 'an autobiographical flour-
ish' in every critical essay—'a gold hoop dangling from the navel
of one's argument'.[30] It is not enough to flash our pierced parts in
a momentary act of self disclosure. 'Reading with' reshapes and
remakes our space and our place. 'Listening to' the narratives
of 'others', especially those 'others' who have had to suffer our
otherness imposed upon them, their 'readings', and resources is
not enough. David Tracy is right, the imperative to listen cannot
be the final word.[31] Our reading practice must be located within a
particular vision of resistance and hope as we collaborate and
work with particular communities of the poor and marginalized.
This too is our place.

Postmodern (and poststructuralist) impulses enable us to make
this move—to relocate.[32] Drawing on these impulses Welch argues
that we can only transcend 'the blinders of our own social
location...by recognizing the differences by which we ourselves
are constituted and...by actively seeking to be partially constituted by work with different groups'.[33] 'Reading with' others in
contexts where we also work with them remakes us. Work with
groups who have been differently constituted exposes us to some
of the forces and factors that have constituted them and enables
us to be partially constituted by them. Recognizing that our
becoming selves are always in the process of being constructed
and negotiated enables us not only 'to articulate and claim a
particular historical and social identity, to locate ourselves' and

---

30. Stephen D. Moore, 'True Confessions and Weird Obsessions: Autobiographical Interventions in Literary and Biblical Studies', *Semeia* 72 (1995),
pp. 19-50 (19).

31. Tracy, *Plurality and Ambiguity*, p. 90.

32. Waugh, *Practising Postmodernism*, pp. 54-61, 114-64; Fulkerson, *Changing the Subject*, pp. 3-116, 355-95.

33. Welch, *A Feminist Ethic*, p. 151.

'to build coalitions from a recognition of the partial knowledges of our own constructed identities',[34] but also offers us ways of becoming other than we are.

Work with poor and marginalized communities enables white, middle-class, male biblical scholars like me to be partially constituted by the experiences, needs, questions and resources of other communities. As I have already said, this does not mean that my 'whiteness', 'middle-classness' and 'maleness' cease to be the major factors that constitute me, but they are no longer the whole story. I will need to be reminded again and again that I am indeed substantially shaped and indelibly inscribed by my whiteness, middle-classness and maleness, but I now know that I need not remain content to be so. I can choose to be other.

As I conclude this chapter I want to stress, again, that what I have called 'reading with'—the reading interface between two vigilantly foregrounded subject positions in which structures are in place through which power relations are acknowledged and mediated—assumes that the Bible is a significant text which is meaningful, powerful and true for the 'readers' who read together. Some socially engaged scholars are of the opinion that the Bible should not be used by the poor and marginalized because it is inherently and thoroughly oppressive. In the ISB our position is different. We have chosen to be partially constituted by the reality of the poor and marginalized communities that call us to read the Bible with them, and that the Bible is meaningful, powerful and true for them is a part of this reality.

In reading with ordinary African 'readers' we have found that our interpretative interests seem to offer additional resources for appropriating parts of the biblical tradition that resonate with the presence of God with them, and for reading against those other parts that have been used to oppress them. We may not always like what they do with our resources, as they transgress the boundaries of our methodologies and use our analytical tools together with their own 'well-crafted weapons' against us and our alienating and dominating interpretations. Their readings do not advocate a methodology—they have more important purposes, they are 'a way of using methodologies'.[35] 'Re-membering', they read with

34. Weiler, 'Feminist Pedagogy', pp. 469-70.
35. Hendricks, 'Guerilla Exegesis', p. 79.

the grain and against the grain, they make syncopated and sub-versive methodological moves to recover subjugated, forgotten and neglected meanings, as they applaud a Jesus who is tricky and debate with a God who is undemocratic.[36]

36. Philpott, *Jesus Is Tricky*.

6 |

The Contextual Bible Study Process:
An Exercise and Further Reflection

This chapter attempts to give readers of this book a feel for the contextual Bible study process, beginning with a simulated reading experience in which readers of this book participate. The reading process in which readers will participate and which I will facilitate has been shaped in the interface between critical biblical scholarship and the readings of a variety of groups of ordinary 'readers' from poor and marginalized communities. This 'workshop' component leads into some further theoretical discussion of aspects of the relationship between Biblical Studies and ordinary 'readers' of the Bible in the church and community. The chapter searches for and probes a reading process that is accountable both to the critical resources of biblical scholarship and the contextual (and critical) resources of various communities of the poor and marginalized.

In no sense in which I use the term are readers of this book 'ordinary readers'! Readers of this volume are critical or post-critical readers of the Bible, whereas ordinary 'readers' read pre-critically. And while ordinary 'readers', in the specific sense in which I usually use the term, are from poor and marginalized sectors of society, only some readers now reading this chapter are from such sectors, and all are probably from the middle-classes. Nevertheless, there are aspects of 'the workshop experience' in which we can participate together.

Let us imagine that our group has invited the Institute for the Study of the Bible (ISB) to work with them during a weekend workshop on the theme 'Liberating Ways of Reading the Bible as Women'. This particular contextual Bible study begins with a question.

Question 1: Read Mk 5.21–6.1 and discuss in small groups what this text is about.

Responses to this question probably include some of the following: healing, compassion, faith, love, hope, despair and many others. Readers could probably extend this list. Some groups may include 'women' as a theme of this text, as did one of the groups of ordinary 'readers' with whom this exercise was done.

Once there has been feedback from each group, and all the responses documented on newsprint, the participants return to their groups for the next two questions of the Bible study.

Question 2: Who are the main characters, and what do we know about them?

This question returns the 'readers' to the text as they try to glean as much as they can about the various characters. What begins to emerge is that this text seems to be about women. This suggestion is supported by a careful reading of the text. First, the story of the two women is a literary unit, delimited by the geographic shifts in vv. 21 and 61. Second, although the central character appears initially to be a man, Jairus, the central characters in the story are in fact two women. Jairus does initiate the action, but is then ignored as first the woman with the flow of blood and then Jairus's daughter move to centre-stage. The actual absence of the first woman mentioned, Jairus's daughter, emphasizes her narrative presence. The plot depends on her presence. Similarly, the woman with the flow of blood, the second woman, is foregrounded even though she seeks to be self-effacing. And while Jesus is still speaking to the second woman, the first woman is again represented by others (v. 35). It is almost as if the narrator himself (herself?) is interrupted—the narrative certainly is—by the unnamed woman with the flow of blood.[1] The careful narrative introduction of Jairus, a named male with power (v. 22) is

---

1.   This woman is named Berenice by some in Latin America; see Soares De Oliveira, 'Feminist Theology in Brazil', p. 66.

first interrupted, and then deconstructed, by the unnamed woman with no power.

Third, that the plot and sub-plot are carefully connected is stressed by the repetition of 'daughter', in v. 34 with reference to the second woman and in v. 35 with reference to the first woman. The ambiguity of 'your daughter', referring to Jairus and possibly to Jesus, in v. 35 reinforces this connection. The women, and so their stories, are also linked by repetition of 'twelve years' (vv. 25 and 42). It has also been suggested by some readers that 'twelve years' may, in the case of the young woman, be an allusion to the onset of menstruation and so the beginning of fertility. The flow of blood for the younger woman meant life was possible, but the flow of blood for the older woman meant that life was no longer possible. The young woman of twelve years of age is a narrative reminder of the child(ren) that the older woman has not been able to bear. Here is another link between the two stories. There is also a parallel structure to each episode. In each case the woman is defined by her social location; in each case the woman is in need; in each case Jesus responds to her need; in each case the woman is unclean; in each case there is contact, touching, between Jesus and the woman; in each case Jesus speaks to the woman; in each case there is healing and restoration of the woman to the community.

While Jesus is always seen as a major character who is on the side of the women, the emerging presence of the women as central characters did sometimes cast him in another light. Some women wondered whether Jesus was not conscientized by the faith of the woman who touched him. Would Jesus have been as radical as he was without this woman? For most women, however, the Jesus of the story is the Jesus who they know and experience as being with them in their daily struggle for survival, liberation and life, and so their focus in the reading is firmly on the women. While the text may be about the things they initially mentioned, they now know it is about women—about them.

At this point in the Bible study the facilitator of the group suggests that it is appropriate to move on to the next question.

Question 3: What are the relationships between the characters and between the characters and their context?

Once again, this question returns participants to the text as they attempt to understand the message. Extensive discussion and digging into the text with a whole range of experiences and resources yield some fruit and some frustration. A partial picture begins to emerge of two women bound by social systems—similar to their own—from which they are liberated by Jesus. Adding to the textual and socio-historical resources of the ordinary 'readers' the socially engaged biblical scholar in the group facilitates further exchange. The partial picture already constructed begins to take on a clearer shape as the responses of the ordinary 'readers' are supported by some input on the sociological setting of these women.

Both women are initially identified in terms of patriarchal social systems, and not in their own right. They are not named, they are described in terms of their location within two interlocking social systems. The first woman is defined by the patriarchal system of first-century Palestine. She is defined in terms of her relationship to a male, her father. The second woman is defined by the purity system of first-century Palestine. She is defined in terms of her uncleanness, her flow of blood. Both women, in other words, are situated in social systems that determine how the world in which they live relates to them.

But Jesus responds differently. Having heard the story of the second woman, he embraces her uncleanness by affirming her faith and healing. Her twelve years of uncleanness and social alienation are ended when she is healed and restored to the community. The acceptance and affirmation of Jesus, together with her faith, bring freedom from her religious, economic (v. 26), sexual and social suffering. The nameless, self-effacing woman has become a part of the Jesus movement, has become 'daughter'. Jesus has literally empowered her (v. 30)! There will still be times when this woman will not be able to worship in the temple, when she will not be able to be touched, when she will be unclean, when she will be marginalized by the patriarchal purity system. But that system has been challenged and changed by her story.

Similarly with the first woman. Not only does Jesus touch her
unclean dead body (v. 41), he also refers to her in her own right
rather than as the property of her father. Her father and 'some
men' (used by certain English translations) refer to her in the
patriarchal genitive (vv. 23 and 35). Jesus relates to the young
woman as a subject, not as an object (vv. 39 and 41). Significantly,
the narrator adopts Jesus' subject designation in v. 40 in his implicit refusal to describe the young woman as the property of her
father, in contrast to the patriarchal positioning language of Jairus
and his men. Instead of defining the young woman as possessed
by her father, as an object (see v. 23 where Jairus refers to her as
'My little daughter'), the narrator now designates her as a subject,
possessing her father and mother (v. 40). There will still be times
when this young woman is defined in terms of her social location
within a patriarchal household, when she will be described with
the possessive case, when she will be treated as an object by the
patriarchal system. But that system has been challenged and
changed by her story.

After reporting back to a plenary gathering of the participants,
people return to their groups for the final question.

Question 4: In what way does this text speak to us today?

This question can only be answered by groups of readers in their
own contexts, so it is perhaps an appropriate time to leave the
limitations of the simulation.

Readers who have actively participated in the workshop exercise
will now have some feel for the contextual Bible study process. In
the actual Bible studies on which this discussion is based there
were a variety of responses to this last question. In one group, for
example, women began to explore ways of lobbying the newly
elected government to make health care for women a priority; as
one of their group had been elected to a government position,
this was a realist line of action. In another group, the women
decided to design a series of Bible studies that would make men in
their congregations more conscious of cultural structures and attitudes that oppress women. All the women experienced the Bible
study as empowering. In the words of one women, while the Bible

still remained contested terrain, 'This Bible study has stopped me from throwing my Bible into the toilet and flushing it away'.

But surely the actual Bible studies did not produce the above reading 'as is'? Some explanation of the process that generated the above critical and contextual reading is needed. The basic shape and substance of the reading emerged from a Bible study with a women's group in Umtata, the urban centre of a vast rural region in the Eastern Province of South Africa. The group consists of a majority of black women, most of whom are from Umtata, with a few from rural areas, and some white women from Umtata. The theme of their workshop was 'Liberating Ways of Reading the Bible as Women'. The ISB was asked to facilitate the workshop.[2]

The theme of the workshop was determined by the Umtata women's group, as well as the programme. The ISB was asked to suggest some texts for Bible study in addition to those selected by the planning committee. The Mark text was one of the texts suggested by us. The text was chosen because two of the main characters are women. Besides this, there was no clear sense of where the Bible study group might go with the text. No exegesis was done in preparation, and the questions used to facilitate the Bible study process were those listed above.

The type of questions used is significant, and we tend to work with two question types. Questions 1 and 4 are examples of what might be called 'community consciousness' questions, and are designed to encourage participants to engage with the text from their own experience. Any response is appropriate to these questions, and a good facilitator will make sure that every response is noted and documented on newsprint for all to see. It is important

---

2.   In a recent workshop on contextual Bible study, participants agreed that the five most important characteristics of a facilitator were the following: the facilitator should use a method that encourages the whole group to participate; the facilitator should manage conflict and make the group a safe place for member contributions; the facilitator should train others to become facilitators; the facilitator should clarify what is not clear and should summarize the discussion; and the facilitator should enable the group to become aware of, and involved in, the needs of the community. A facilitator, then, is one who helps the progress and empowerment of others, who makes it easier for others to act, to contribute, and to acquire skills. See Gerald O. West, *Contextual Bible Study* (Pietermaritzburg: Cluster Publications, 1993).

that the contextual Bible study process begins and ends with such questions as they enable participants to 'own' the process. This type of question allows for an initial articulation of what is incipient and inchoate, however tentative and however much such an articulation may be couched in the terms of the dominant, orthodox, discourse. Questions 2 and 3 are examples of 'critical consciousness' questions, what Cornel West calls 'enabling forms of criticism',[3] which ask for a more critical response to the text, and which create a measure of distance between 'reader' and the text. By facilitating a close and careful reading of the text and by exploring the relationship between the text and its socio-historical context, the text as literary and socio-cultural artifact is taken seriously. In a variety of ways such questions draw out the critical resources of both ordinary 'readers' and socially engaged biblical scholars, and enable a critical appropriation.

Although the reading I have described had its beginning in the Umtata workshop, the process that produced this reading did not end there. Subsequent to the Umtata women's workshop, a local Anglican church asked me to preach on the subject of 'Compassion and Women'. Having expressed some disquiet at being asked, as a male, to do this, I declined to preach, but offered to do a short workshop instead. The same format was used as with the Umtata women's group, but this time the ordinary readers were mainly white, about 60 per cent women and 40 per cent men. These participants are only 'ordinary readers' in a general sense, and not in my specific sense. They have not been trained to use the tools and strategies of biblical scholarship, so are ordinary readers in this sense; however, most are not from poor and marginalized communities. My commitment to the contextual Bible study process entailed approaching this workshop from the perspective of the poor and marginalized, and so I used the experiences and the responses of the women from the Umtata workshop as a way into the workshop. This seemed to create space for the women in the congregation to take a more active role in the workshop than they usually do in congregation gatherings. Their responses too have shaped the reading presented here.

3.   Cornel West, *Prophetic Fragments* (Grand Rapids: Eerdmans, 1988), p. 210.

I then did a workshop with a Master's class in the School of Theology, University of Natal, Pietermaritzburg. It is part of my pedagogical practice to use such resources with students.[4] This time the responses of trained and semi-trained readers were allowed to shape the Bible study, but only in ways that were 'accountable' to the shape that had emerged 'from below'. This was not difficult or forced because most of the responses of these trained readers, half of whom are women and most of whom come from poor and marginalized communities, supported and strengthened the reading of the ordinary 'readers'. The readings of these trained and semi-trained readers might have been more structured and systematic, but the contextual Bible study process produced substantially similar responses, beginning as each did with the categories and concepts contributed by the women of the Umtata workshop.

The final phase in the development of the reading rendered in this chapter included some additional systematic structuring and further textual and sociological support for the reading that had already emerged from the contextual Bible study process. But as I continue to work with this text with other groups of ordinary 'readers' I am constantly amazed at how much I still have to learn from them. There is no final reading product, only an account of some of the readings I have been able to participate in and to reflect on. So I do not want to place undue emphasis on the reading product; implicit in *the process* we have participated in are a number of elements which need to be articulated explicitly, and which will act as a reminder of aspects previously discussed.

Contextual Bible study begins with the needs and concerns of poor and marginalized communities. The question or questions that shape the Bible reading emerge from below, not from above. So in actual contextual readings of Mk 5.21–6.1, on which this exercise and this chapter are based, the life interests of the participating group determined the generative theme,[5] and in each case the theme focused on 'women'. Socially engaged biblical scholars did not dictate the theme, it was elicited from the life experience

4. See Gerald O. West, 'Power and Pedagogy in a South African Context: A Case Study in Biblical Studies', *Academic Development* 2 (1996), pp. 47-65.

5. See Paulo Freire, *Pedagogy of the Oppressed* (New York: Continuum, 1970).

of ordinary 'readers'. Because the ISB is committed to working with organized communities or groups who can 'talk back' and who have the identity, structures and resources to 'own' the workshop process, the overall direction for and of the workshop is independent of our participation.

Within such a framework of accountability to Bible study groups of ordinary 'readers', socially engaged biblical scholars can participate fully in the Bible study process. By deliberately choosing to work in those contexts in which it is possible for subject positions and power relations to be vigilantly foregrounded, the reading interface in which socially engaged biblical scholars and ordinary 'readers' participate is subject to subject—is 'reading with'. So when we are invited to participate we can do so without being apologetic about the reading resources we bring with us. So, for example, in each of the three workshops I felt able to suggest that this text, along with a number of other texts identified by the groups, might be relevant to the chosen theme. The advantage of a text like Mk 5.21–6.1 is that is not usually perceived as a text primarily about women. Consequently, reading familiar texts in different ways 'surprises' ordinary 'readers' and offers unexpected 'lines of connection'. Previously 'tamed' and 'domesticated' texts take on a new disclosive potential as received readings are rejected and new possibilities explored.

In addition to offering alternative resources for reading familiar texts, socially engaged biblical scholars can introduce unknown, neglected and abandoned texts—texts from the margins of the Bible—to the reading process. The danger with well-known texts is that they already have strong reception histories and marked effects, and it is not always easy to read against the damage they have done. So, for example, in other workshops where the theme has had to do with women, we have suggested texts like 2 Sam. 13.1-22 and 2 Sam. 21.1-14, which are seldom, if ever, read.[6] The very presence of a text like 2 Sam. 13.1-22 creates space for women to speak about things not usually spoken of in church and to break the culture of silence about violence against women.[7]

6.   I will discuss the latter text in Chapter 8.
7.   For a detailed account of how ordinary African women worked with this text (and others texts) see *Report of the ISB Biennial Workshop: Women and*

In any reading of the Bible in the interface between trained and ordinary 'readers' there is a great deal that ordinary 'readers' can discover and recover in texts using their own resources, provided there is some facilitation of this process. So in each of the three workshops the Bible was read communally, in small groups, with each group appointing a facilitator. The primary role of facilitator is to enable 'group process' to take place—to manage group dynamics, to promote turn taking, to keep time, to summarize and systematize the reading results, to find creative and empowering ways of reporting back to plenary the findings of the group,[8] and to move the group from reflection into action. Beside the more general group process concerns, the facilitator's task in the contextual Bible study process is to stimulate the use of local reading resources and to introduce critical reading resources—in the specific sense that this term is used within biblical studies—into the reading process as they are requested and required. This is no easy task, and so much of the work of the ISB involves training facilitators in local communities. Contextual Bible study, then, is committed to corporate and communal reading of the Bible in which the trained reader is just another reader with *different* resources and skills, *not better* resources and skills. As I have argued, really believing that our modes of reading are 'different, but not better' requires some form of conversion. Remaining within the categories and concepts of ordinary 'readers', resisting

the Bible in South and Southern Africa (Pietermaritzburg: ISB, 1996). Copies of this report can be obtained from me.

8.   In a Bible study on the theme 'Women and Healing'—it should be clear by now that the ISB is often invited to work with women—we used 2 Kgs 5.1-19a as one of the texts to be read. The questions used in the Bible study were the following: 1. Read 2 Kgs 5.1-19a in your own translation. What is the text about? 2. Who are the main characters in the story and what do we know about each of them? 3. What is the basic plot of the story? Draw a simple plot line which indicates how the story develops. 4. What is the untold story of the the young slave girl who is the key agent in this story? Try and be creative in your 're-telling'; e.g. write a letter from the young slave girl to her family, compose a poem, perform a drama, sing a song, find a flower, etc. 5. What untold stories in your context does your 'telling' bring to your memory? Tell their stories to the group. 6. What will you do in response to this Bible study? Question 4 offered opportunities for wonderfully creative and empowering responses.

the temptation to 'translate' local articulations in the terms of the dominant discourse,[9] takes considerable conversion, and careful facilitation.

I have already drawn attention to the importance of critical resources for reading within the contextual Bible study process. While ordinary 'readers' do have critical resources, these are not the specific critical resources of biblical scholarship. Creative facilitation can offer ordinary readers a wider range of critical resources than they usually have access to.[10] In our reading of Mk 5.21–6.1 I concentrated on providing resources from two particular forms of critical reading. A close and careful—literary—mode of reading was used to explore the characters and the internal relationships within the text. The use of narrative transitions to delimit the literary unit (which is why we read from 5.21 to 6.1), the reading of the whole text to discern its structure, the careful and close reading of the component parts, the return to reread the text as a whole in the light of the reading of the parts, and the continual attention to the internal relationships within the text, including reference to plot, character, setting, theme, rhetorical devices like repetition, and other literary aspects, are all elements of this mode of reading. While ordinary 'readers' in the workshops were not familiar with these literary resources for reading in any systematic way, they were able with relative ease to recognize and appreciate their usefulness and to integrate these resources into their own modes of reading.

When questions from the group required it, a socio-historical mode of reading was used to situate this text in its first century context. The implicit use of historical-critical tools to delimit the text and to locate it historically, and the reconstruction of aspects of the sociological world that produced the text, including reference to the patriarchal and purity systems of first-century Pales-

---

9. See the useful distinction between emic and etic analysis in Mark G. Brett, 'Four or Five Things to Do with Texts: A Taxonomy of Interpretative Interests', in David J.A. Clines, Stephen E. Fowl and Stanley E. Porter (eds.), *The Bible in Three Dimensions: Essays in Celebration of Forty Years of Biblical Studies in the University of Sheffield* (JSOTSup, 87; Sheffield: Sheffield Academic Press, 1990), pp. 357-77. An emic description uses the categories and concepts of the local community being analysed, whereas an etic description uses categories and concepts external to the local community being analysed.

10. Draper and West, 'Anglicans and Scripture', pp. 39-44.

tine, are elements of this mode of reading. Once again, while ordinary 'readers' were not familiar with these historical and sociological resources, they were able with relative ease to recognize and appreciate their usefulness and to integrate these resources into their own modes of reading.

It must be stressed again that these critical resources were not used as the way into the text. The Bible study began with the social interests of the participants. The generative theme determined by the group provided the entry point and activated the existing reading resources of the group. Such a thematic entry into the text provides for many forms of engagement with the text, including the experiences, needs, questions and resources of the participants, and establishes a local conceptual framework for the Bible study. So the contextual Bible study always begins with reality as it is perceived by poor and marginalized participants. Because critical modes of reading tend to create some distance between readers and text they come second and serve whatever resources and readings are already present. However, the often urgent demands of the context usually hold forms of engagement and forms of critical distance together in a creative dialectic;[11] the tentative testing and articulating of 'working' readings (and theologies) seems to require the use of both local community resources for reading and critical modes of reading.

The range of experience and reading resources that groups of ordinary 'readers' bring to their reading of the Bible is various and vast. Creative facilitation, including asking questions instead of simply providing information, draws on their experiences and resources and in so doing empowers them to construct their own critical and contextual readings. Ordinary 'readers' from poor and marginalized communities have no problem being contextual,[12] and they eagerly, if erratically and eclectically, take up the additional resources brought by socially engaged biblical scholars to the reading process. The contextual Bible study process is not simply a naive and romantic 'listening to', nor is it a paternalistic and marginalizing 'reading for'; it is a process in which we 'read with' each other, where we vigilantly foreground our respective

11. For a fuller discussion of the relationship between engagement, critical distance, and context see West, 'Power and Pedagogy'.

12. Draper and West, 'Anglicans and Scripture', p. 43.

subject positions and where we become explicit concerning the power relations implicit in the reading process.

The key contribution of critical resources to the contextual Bible study process seems to be that it enables ordinary readers themselves to articulate what is incipient—to give shape to what is inchoate. While the first response in many Bible study groups is often, as the responses to Question 1 show, the 'missionary response' or the dogmatically 'correct' response—the public transcript—critical modes of reading enable ordinary people from poor and marginalized communities to begin to articulate readings and theologies that are incipient, if it is safe to do so. What is hidden from the dominant is hidden for good reason, and can and should only be openly spoken in a context of trust and accountability. But within such a context, the intersection of community resources and the critical resources of biblical scholarship enables the recognizing, the recovering and the reviving and arousing of what is inchoate and incipient—the dangerous memories and subjugated knowledges that constitute the hidden transcript.

What Scott's analysis has helped us to understand is why there is this remarkable readiness on the part of ordinary 'readers' in poor and marginalized communities to use the critical resources of biblical scholarship. Because the hidden transcript is never a language apart, but is in constant dialogue—or more accurately, in constant argument—with the dominant discourse, and because the argument demands a presence in the public transcript, it must of necessity 'borrow heavily from the terms of the dominant ideology prevailing in the public transcript'.[13] But in the artful hands of the dominated, the dominant discourse 'is capable of carrying an enormous variety of meanings, including those that are subversive of their use as intended by the dominant'.[14] Through the contextual Bible study process, it would seem, the poor and marginalized do with the Bible and its dominant readings and receptions what they routinely do with the dominant discourse—they 're-member' it. Having already forged tools and strategies for dealing with the dominant discourse—'re-membering' resources—they readily take up the additional resources

13. Scott, *Domination*, p. 102.
14. Scott, *Domination*, pp. 102-103.

biblical scholarship offers them for their 're-membering' of the Bible, both as they deal with it directly and in their encounters with the dominant readings and receptions of it.

Because the oral culture of subordinate groups is the primary domain in which the dismembering and 're-membering' of the dominant discourse takes place, they are less familiar with the textual dimensions of 're-membering'. Because orality offers seclusion, control and anonymity, it is an ideal vehicle for ideological resistance. Each enactment is unique as to time, place and audience, as well as different from every other enactment. Gossip, rumour, folktales, songs, gestures, jokes and theatre—the terrain of orality and the zone of the hidden transcript—are taken up, performed or learned at the option of the listeners and, over time, their origins are lost altogether.

> It becomes impossible to recover some *ur* version from which all subsequent renditions are deviations. In other words, there is no orthodoxy or center to folk culture since there is no primary text to serve as the measure of heresy. The practical result is that folk culture achieves the anonymity of collective property, constantly being adjusted, revised, abbreviated, or, for that matter, ignored. The multiplicity of its authors provides its protective cover, and when it no longer serves current interests sufficiently to find performers or an audience, it simply vanishes forever.[15]

The advantage of oral communication (including gestures, clothes, dance, and so on) 'is that the communicator retains control over the manner of its dissemination—the audience, the place, the circumstances, the rendition. Control, then, of oral culture is irretrievably decentralized.'[16]

Resistance does also take place on the textual terrain, with written forms of communication providing considerable anonymity and flexibility. However, as biblical scholars well know, once a text is out of the author's hands, control over its interpretation, use, and dissemination is lost. So while subordinates do make use of text among their forms of resistance, it is not a familiar medium. The Bible as text, therefore, poses peculiar problems for poor and marginalized 'readers'. Most ordinary African 'readers' are more

15. Scott, *Domination*, p. 161.
16. Scott, *Domination*, p. 161.

familiar with the Bible as symbol—the 'unopened' Bible,[17] or with the heard and remembered Bible; such forms are more easily manipulated and 're-membered'. So when it comes to the 'opened' Bible—the Bible as text—ordinary 'readers' eagerly embrace the resources offered by socially engaged biblical scholars, in order to 're-member' the text.

In so doing they discover lines of connection with a whole host of previously hidden locations. They find, for example, that the text we have been reading in this chapter can be read as a text about women, even though they have never heard it being read in this way before. They discover, in other words, that the resisting stories of their sisters are discernible in the discourse of the dominant, just as their own resisting stories are discernible in the discourses of the public transcripts, provided one has an ear to hear. For example, one of the most common forms of veiled cultural resistance of subordinate groups is the trickster tale. Typically, tricksters make their way successfully through a treacherous and dangerous environment of enemies out to defeat—or eat—them, not by their strength but by their wit and cunning. Tricksters are unable, in principle, to win any direct confrontation as they are smaller and weaker than their antagonists. Only by knowing the habits of their enemies, by deceiving them, by taking advantage of their haste, greed, size and gullibility, do they manage to escape the clutches of the enemy and win victories.[18]

Trickster tales, like the Brer Rabbit tales of African (American) slaves, are not only told offstage in the slave quarters, they are also a part of the public transcript, and demonstrate the tremendous desire and will of subordinate groups to express publicly what is in the hidden transcript, even if that form of expression must use metaphors and allusions in the interest of safety.[19] Because they are thus veiled, trickster tales may find a permanent place in the public record. Such may be the case with the well-known story of Isaac, Rebekah, Esau and Jacob in Genesis 27. What was probably a trickster tale, told by women,[20] has been taken up, by an

17. See the discussion in Chapter 4.
18. Scott, *Domination*, p. 162.
19. Scott, *Domination*, p. 163.
20. See A.J. Bledstein, 'Binder, Trickster, Heel and Hairy-man: Rereading

unsuspecting or calculating author or redactor, and has become part of a larger patriarchal narrative. A female story has been co-opted by the fathers! The female trickster is now a character in an extended story which is obviously a story about male matters, including lineage, succession, blessing and inheritance. However, 'a more nuanced and literary reading' can detect the trickster tale that celebrates the guile and cleverness of the woman Rebekah. This apparently innocuous tale, which has enough to do with androcentric concerns to be tolerated in the public record, provides other women with a protagonist who manages to outwit and ridicule her more powerful adversary.

Within this relatively veiled context women have a vehicle that expresses *publicly* a form of resistance. Such tales would not only be told offstage in the women's quarters as a way of socializing a spirit of resistance, they would also have a place in public discourse because of their disguise. The story has a form which is both acceptable to men and empowering of women. Clearly, such a tale also has an instructive and cautionary side. Identifying with Rebekah, women, including young women, learn that in a context of overwhelming male domination safety and success often depend upon channelling resistance into forms of deception and cunning. While it may seem 'that the heavy disguise this reply wears must all but eliminate the pleasure it gives', it nevertheless 'carves out a public, if provisional, space for the autonomous cultural expression of dissent. If it is disguised, it is at least not hidden; it is spoken to power. This is no small achievement of voice under domination.'[21]

However, this trickster tale has almost been lost to us because it has been inserted into a larger literary context which is so completely concerned with male matters that we easily miss this form of female resistance. The hidden transcript has had to disguise itself and to speak warily, and so reading resistance from the public and oral traditions of subordinate groups, particularly when these have been incorporated into a larger more ideologically diverse written corpus, requires 'a more nuanced and literary

Genesis 27 as a Trickster Tale Told by a Woman' (unpublished paper, SBL, 1991).

21. Scott, *Domination*, pp. 164-66.

reading'.[22] This is the danger of the written text. But this is also an opportunity for the intellectual, in this case the socially engaged biblical scholar, whose terrain is the text, to serve the poor and marginalized. With the aid of the textual resources of the socially engaged biblical scholar, the Bible becomes more malleable in the hands of ordinary 'readers', enabling them both to locate the marginalized voices in the text and to articulate and 'own' their own incipient and inchoate interpretations.

In KwaZulu-Natal, as elsewhere among the poor and marginalized, the hidden transcript constantly 'presses against and tests the limits of what may be safely ventured in terms of a reply to the public transcript of deference and conformity'. And when the conditions that constrain the readings and theologies of the poor and marginalized are relaxed, as they have been in certain sectors in South Africa, 'we may expect to see [as indeed we are] the disguises become less opaque as more of the hidden transcript shoulders its way onto the stage and into action'.[23] So as the hegemony of the apartheid state and its religious ideology, 'Church theology',[24] are beginning to weaken, there has been a growing eagerness and boldness not only to speak what has been hidden and disguised—to shout 'what has historically been whispered, controlled, choked back, stifled, and suppressed'[25]—but also *to own* what is liberating and life giving. The power of an articulation that resonates with what is incipient and inchoate in others and that then becomes the social property of the group is phenomenal. For example, in one of the groups with which we regular work in an informal settlement, the leaders approached the ISB to arrange for them to learn English so that they could enter national ecumenical structures and 'speak for ourselves'.

22. Scott, *Domination*, p. 165.
23. Scott, *Domination*, p. 172.
24. See *The Kairos Document*.
25. Scott, *Domination*, p. 227. If the results of the declaration of the hidden transcript 'seem like moments of madness, if the politics they engender is tumultuous, frenetic, delirious, and occasionally violent, that is perhaps because the powerless are so rarely on the public stage and have so much to say and do when they finally arrive'.

Contextual Bible study provides processes, resources and a place for the making and shaping that is a part of owning. It facilitates a more systematic and structured articulation of what is incipient and inchoate, the purpose of which is to effect transformation and change. The final question in the simulated workshop was *In what way does this text speak to us today?* The reading resources of the contextual Bible study process provide ordinary 'readers' with the tools and strategies to situate the text both within its literary and linguistic context and within its socio-historical and cultural context, and in so doing enables them (and us) to appropriate the text more critically. Situating the text in these ways prevents a simple correspondence between text and present context. The Bible still speaks, but it speaks more cautiously. That it speaks, and ordinary 'readers' in the African context do not doubt this, encourages the socially engaged biblical scholar to complete the hermeneutic cycle and risk appropriation, albeit a critical appropriation. We must not pretend to be content with 'what it meant', making covert connections with our social agendas; we must move on to asking 'what it means', becoming explicit about our social interests and allowing our agendas to be know by others. The final commitment of the contextual Bible study process is to read the Bible for individual and social transformation—describing, even analysing, what is, is not enough; we must risk deciding for a particular plan of action—for what might be.

The readings produced in this interface probably affect ordinary and trained 'readers' differently, which is not surprising. We come to the text from different places and after the reading encounter return to our different places. Our subjectivities are differently constituted, and so the effect that the corporate reading process and product has on us and our respective contexts will be different. However, and this is extremely important, we will have been partially constituted by each other. This is perhaps the most enduring and transfiguring contribution of 'reading with' for people like me—that I become other by being partially constituted by 'others' from poor and marginalized communities. Rooted as it is in both a community consciousness and a critical consciousness, contextual Bible study provides resources for 'a theoretically well-grounded and culturally autonomous' discourse.[26] Resisting, liberating and life-giving resources are found in our 'belonging in difference'.

The finished product which is the reading presented here in this chapter, as is the case with all the readings in the book, was not produced by ordinary 'readers'. It is in this form my reading. It had its beginnings among ordinary black women who were struggling to hear God speak to their needs and questions, but it remains my re-presentation. What they have taken away from the Bible study workshop and how they will use it, I do not fully know. For example, one of the woman in the Umtata women's group summed up her group's discussion with the words: 'The problem is that men don't bleed; men must bleed!' What this means for that group of women and what they will do with this reading is theirs; it belongs to them and their communities. I am content with this and have no desire for surveillance or control. I have gleaned from them, and through this book I am able to share with you glimpses of readings that are to be found offstage among the poor and marginalized which call us to share their struggle with the God of life against the forces of death. At other times and in other places they will speak for themselves, but not in this book (though perhaps the next chapter gives them some real presence). In this book they remain re-presented.

26. Mosala, *Black Theology*, pp. 2-3.

7 |

Reading Other-wise: A Case Study

The experience of participating in a contextual Bible study in the previous chapter has probably been overwhelmed by the commentary and analysis that followed the exercise. So here I offer the reader an opportunity to observe an actual contextual Bible study.

This Bible study is one of a series of Bible studies which took place on a regular, weekly basis in an informal settlement near Pietermaritzburg and Durban. Most of these Bible studies, over a period of more than six years, have been recorded, transcribed and translated into English (from Zulu). Thirteen of them are included in a remarkable reflection on the Bible studies by Graham Philpott.[1] Contextual Bible studies and a range of related activities still continue in Amawoti among various sectors of the community.

I have chosen a Bible study that I observed, but did not participate in directly, and which I think incorporates many of the features I have been discussing in this book. But I will resist offering an exegesis of or even a commentary on this Bible study. I invite the reader to enter this interface without me as guide, and to find there what may be found. I realize that this is not an easy thing to do, but I hope that you will stop for a while and enter this place where socially engaged biblical scholars are welcome. While there may not be a place for us who read together in this way in the inn of the academy, there is plenty of space in the shacks of Amawoti.

I cannot resist, however, pointing out that this Bible study demonstrates that contextual Bible study is not a method, either in the sense of a set procedure in which certain steps are followed, or in the sense of a particular mode of reading being used.

1. Philpott, *Jesus Is Tricky*, pp. 136-98.

Contextual Bible study is more of consciousness, a set of commitments, an orientation. My work has been to try to discern the patterns in that vast array of encounters that we call contextual Bible study. Perhaps you will recognize some of these patterns in this Bible study (or deconstruct them!).

This Bible study took place on 28 October 1988. The participants are Mbuso, Philani, Phumzile, Zithulele, Sandile, Nomonde, Dombi, Sara and Sipho (who is the facilitator). The passage they are discussing is Lk. 4.16-22.

Sipho opened the discussion with prayer. He then gave an introduction to the passage to be discussed, saying that it was Jesus' first sermon which describes the purpose of his coming to earth.

Sipho: Why do you think Christ came to earth?

Silence.

Dombi: To show us the way to heaven.

Dombi read the passage.

Sipho described the sequence of events as they occur in the passage, explaining how Jesus came to be at the synagogue and what would have been expected of him there.

Sandile: What is a synagogue?
Phumzile: It's a Jewish Church.

Sipho continued with explaining how Christ would have read from the scroll from Isaiah, and then sat down to speak.

Sipho: In Amawoti people stand to pray as a sign of respect—as we did at the community high school last year.
Sandile: Like the Roman [Catholic] Church—they kneel.
Mbuso: Like the Anglicans—they also kneel.
Sipho: Then Christ sits down in order to preach. Christ says that today this prophecy from Isaiah will come true.
Philani: Did Jesus go to school?
Phumzile: He must have learnt somewhere because he knew how to read.
Sara: His parents must have taught him. The Jews have the ceremony called the Bar Mitzvah.
Sipho: They probably didn't have schools like we have today, but he would have learnt how to read by learning the law and the commandments. He certainly had no university training.
Sandile: It was just natural intelligence.

Sipho: The most important verses are 18 and 19, the ones he read from Isaiah.

Sipho reads the verses in Zulu, and Sandile translates them into English.

Sipho: Let's discuss verses 18 and 19. Is there anything inter-esting or surprising, or something you are not sure about?

Sandile: I am not sure what Jesus means when he says that he was sent to announce freedom for those who are kidnapped.

Sipho: The translation in English is 'to set the prisoners free'.

Sandile: Did Jesus really do all these things—like making the blind to see?

Philani: Yes, he did.

Sandile: (*With amazement*) He can make blind people see?

Sipho: There are a few passages that refer to Christ healing the blind.

Philani: There was that one man who was shouting 'Son of David'!

Sipho: In verse 18, Jesus says he came to preach good news to the poor. Who are the poor?

Sandile: Those who have nothing. Rich people don't respond to God.

Philani: Some can respond.

Sandile: Yes, only some. If you preach to the poor you will always have a lot of people following you. The poor need to have hope but the rich are comfortable as they are, and are not interested in Jesus.

Philani: Is it wrong to be rich?

Sandile: Rich people are proud.

Sipho: What about Philani's question?

Sandile: It's not wrong—but the rich keep to themselves and they are proud. They are not interested in the poor.

Sipho: So how could Christ bring good news to the poor?

Mbuso: Because Jesus was poor.

Sandile: He had experienced the problems of the poor, and people would listen to him because he was the son of Joseph, an ordinary man.

Sipho: People remembered Jesus' family, and they were amazed to hear him talking like this. The next question is—why are people poor?

Philani: There are many reasons. It could be unemployment, or they don't have money.

Mbuso: Do you mean nowadays or in Jesus' time?

Sipho: Both.

Sandile: Why are you poor Zithulele? Why are you poor Nomonde?

Nomonde: (*Feeling uncomfortable with the question*) I don't have money to buy the things I need.

Dombi:	You must ask Mr Botha [the then apartheid State President] that question. We are poor because of the government.
Mbuso:	But people are also poor because their family has not planned for them—they have not made arrangements for them.
Nomonde:	How can you plan when you are poor?
Sandile:	Even if you plan it is no use—if you don't have a good education then you will always be poor.
Mbuso:	It is possible for a family to provide for their children. They can sell some cows and make sure their children receive an education.
Nomonde:	That's a miracle, if it ever happens!
Sipho:	Where will the child receive an education?
Mbuso:	In South Africa.

Laughter from the group.

Sandile:	You can't receive a good education in South Africa—it is all linked to the government.
Philani:	But there are some people who are rich in the community—like Ngcobo, who owns a big store here.
Dombi:	What happens if you don't have cattle to sell?
Sipho:	Some people get rich by doing well in business.
Sandile:	Ngcobo is an individual case. Let's rather look at poverty among the people.
Mbuso:	If Mr Botha gives equal chances to everybody, will we all be rich?
Sipho:	Not all of us, but more.
Philani:	Even some whites are poor.
Dombi:	If they are poor they must want to be poor!

Laughter.

Sandile:	If a child runs away from school he is kidding himself—he can't get employment without education.
Sipho:	If we look at the whole of Amawoti there are very few people who are rich.
Dombi:	We can even count them—like the Mthembus—they have electricity.
Sandile:	It is a very small percentage—only about 10 families out of l00,000 people.
Sipho:	Let's concentrate rather on the majority: why are they poor? Who controls their education?
Dombi:	You can be educated and still be poor.
Sandile:	If you have an education you will always be able to find a

	job. Your job will be much more secure—they can't tell you just to leave.
Mbuso:	But a labourer can also have a secure job.
Sandile:	They can tell a labourer he's fired whenever they want and there is always someone to replace him. But if you are educated the employer owes you something.
Sipho:	So, what are the reasons why people are poor? We have said that some people don't try; others don't receive a good education because it is controlled by the government; others are poor because of oppression.
Mbuso:	They are oppressed by the rich.
Sipho:	That's right, the rich oppress the poor in order to stay rich.
Sandile:	The rich want to be richer.
Zilhulele:	And the poor want to get poorer!
Sipho:	We all want to get richer.
Mbuso:	How can the poor get richer?
Dombi:	They must pray for God to help them.
Sandile:	There is no manna today.
Philani:	This passage could also mean something different. It could mean poor in a different sense, because Jesus didn't come to give money. He didn't just give food to people.
Sandile:	In those days people weren't relying on money. So Jesus didn't need to bring money. They were relying on crops.
Mbuso:	What else did Jesus bring?
Dombi:	Where did Jesus get money from? Who paid him?
Sandile:	He got it from his job as a carpenter.
Dombi:	But he wasn't supporting his family—and he was thirty years old.
Sipho:	He was working with his father until he was thirty, and then he travelled around during his ministry and was given food by different families.
Philani:	They must have had some money because Judas was the treasurer.
Sandile:	Was Judas the treasurer? I didn't know that! People were very active in ancient times.
Sipho:	Philani was saying that 'poor' means something else. What did you mean Philani?
Philani:	You can be rich with cars and lots of things, but…I don't know how to explain it.
Mbuso:	Yes, you can be rich for this world, but poor on the side of God.
Sipho:	Some people say that you can be poor spiritually although you are rich physically or materially.

Philani: If you are rich spiritually you will always be happy and praising God, no matter what your situation is.

Mbuso: If you are rich you have no time for God and 'me' is on the chair or throne of your life.

Sipho: So, there are two senses of the word 'poor'?

Mbuso: Who did Jesus come for of the two?

Sipho: What do you think?

Mbuso: Both. God cares for everybody. Some people who are poor spiritually believe in Christ.

Sandile: In what way?

Sipho: He came for both. Which one is more important?

Sandile: Those who are poor spiritually.

Mbuso: All are equal in God's eyes. Some people are poor spiritually and have nothing physically.

Sandile: Yes, like the people in Amaotana [a particularly poor section of Amawoti] who are busy drinking.

Sipho: In the past the Church has understood this verse differently. They understood the poor as only the spiritually poor—this was because the leaders of the Church were rich and not part of the poor people. But now there has been a change and some parts of the Church, especially in South America where there is a lot of oppression, have understood the poor to mean the physically poor and the spiritually poor. We need to remember both.

Sandile: Who is Jesus referring to when he talks about prisoners?

Mbuso: People who don't believe in God and are prisoners of Satan.

Sandile: So he is not referring to real prisoners?

Mbuso: He must be referring to both. Satan can have control of both.

Sandile: The leaders in Jesus' time used to ask a lot of questions in order to criticize him.

Sipho: Nowadays who are the prisoners?

Sandile: Those who are oppressed.

Mbuso: Well, last week Bonginkosi and others [leaders of Inkatha] were arrested. Now they are prisoners.

Philani: What! Is Jesus going to release them! [Philani was attacked by the Inkatha vigilantes the previous night.]

There is rejection of this from the group: 'Is Jesus going to release them? No, never! I wouldn't like it if Jesus released them.'

Sipho: Who else are prisoners today?

Mbuso: Another prisoner from Amawoti is Peter Mkhize—he was detained by the SADF on Wednesday. [He was detained by the South African Defence Force on the day of the apartheid elections, 26 October 1988.]

Sandile: But that is different. I think in Jesus' time the system was different. A criminal was punished straightaway. Like if he was a thief, his arm was cut off—that was his punishment. He didn't go to prison. So Bonginkosi would have been executed straight away for all his murders. But Jesus would release Peter Mkhize, because he hadn't really committed a crime, but was just being exploited.

Sipho: The people who were in prison were those who couldn't pay their debts, who owed people money. They were slaves. These are the poor—these are the ones Jesus was going to set free.

Sandile: So the rich people would have complained—who is going to do our work for us?

Sipho: This is different from Bonginkosi—if he has killed somebody then there would be a punishment for that—he wouldn't spend a long time in prison.

Philani: Did Jesus release these prisoners—those owing money and the slaves?

Sandile: Jesus told them that they would be free. By educating people you make people aware of their oppression and slavery.

Philani: Did Jesus come to tell people to riot?

Sandile: No, but to make them realize what their situation is, and to tell the rich people to forgive those who owed them debts.

Mbuso: What about for Bonginkosi? Jesus came for him too. Jesus died together with two criminals. One recognized him as God, and Jesus saved him. The other criminal didn't want to change and mocked Jesus. He was a prisoner of Satan.

Sandile: The second thief didn't realize who Jesus was.

Sipho: If Bonginkosi recognized Jesus and trusted in him, then Jesus would be prepared to forgive him.

Philani: So he would still be a prisoner physically, but Jesus would forgive him.

Sipho: What about the blind?

Sandile: We all have eyes but can't see, and we all have ears but can't hear.

Philani: But Jesus did it practically. For example Mr Khuzwayo was healed from blindness. Who did it?

Sipho: Does Satan have the power to heal the blind?

Sandile: Satan can make you blind but he won't make you see.

Sipho: Yes he can.

Philani:	For example, look what Satan did to Job—he caused diseases, but he doesn't have permission to take a life.
Sandile:	Who are the blind?
Mbuso:	They are the really blind and others. For example, if I share the gospel with you, Sandile, but you don't want to listen, it's like being blind.
Sandile:	By studying the Bible we come to understand, like taking away your blindness.
Mbuso:	To see and also to do.
Sipho:	So it's to understand what God is doing, and to follow him.
Mbuso:	Jesus also preached to people who were not blind.
Sipho:	Let's go to the next part. Who are the oppressed?
Sandile:	I think it is better to ask: who is oppressing me?
Mbuso:	You oppress yourself when you don't want to listen.
Philani:	You can be oppressed by Satan.
Sipho:	The Bible is not only spiritual. It has something to do with earth, with the world. We should first look for the meaning we understand, then look for other meanings. What does oppression mean for us in South Africa today?
Sandile:	We are being oppressed by other humans.
Mbuso:	But those humans are being oppressed by Satan.
Philani:	Then the source of the oppression is Satan.
Mbuso:	So Satan is on top, then the government, then different political parties, then the rich people like Robert Majola [a KwaZulu leader in Inanda, a nearby area]. Then under him are people like Mr Sithole [a local businessman]. These are all the oppressors.
Sandile:	Sithole can be an oppressor because he is not paying enough to people who work for him.
Mbuso:	This is all the chain of oppression.
Sipho:	Behind it all is Satan. Let's look at verse 19. This is called the year of the Jubilee.

Sipho gives a description of Jubilee, and what it meant to the Jewish people— the end of slavery, the end of debt, and families returning to the land originally belonging to them. He gives a contemporary example relating to the rural home of one of the group members.

Sipho:	All this meant a new start, and everything was forgiven.
Mbuso:	(*Amazed*) And there were no problems!
Sipho:	It stopped the rich from getting richer and the poor from getting poorer. In the fiftieth year they could not grow any crops—they had to trust God. God was in control of their society.

Mbuso &	
Sandile:	It's unbelievable!
Sipho:	If Christ came to do this, did he finish doing it? No, not completely. But Jesus started and we must continue.
Philani:	How can we release prisoners?
Mbuso:	By telling them the word of God.
Sandile:	Not only that.
Sipho:	It's similar to Philani's question—how do you preach good news to the poor?
Sandile:	How do you preach in Amaotana?
Philani:	Jesus did a miracle of feeding thousands of people, but after that people just wanted to see the miracles. In the same way, we can't just give people food.
Sandile:	It is important to look at resources. People with no food should learn to plough and grow their own.
Philani:	What about telling them about God?
Dombi:	Tell them about doomsday.
Sandile:	How can you preach the Bible at Amaotana?
Philani:	They must know you before you can preach. They must trust you.
Sipho:	Must you be rich or poor in order to speak to them?
Mbuso:	It is better to be poor.
Philani:	Then if you have a car you must sell it.
Sandile:	There is a saying: 'Give a man a fish and you feed him for one day. If you teach him how to fish, you will feed him for the rest of his life.' This is part of the gospel.
Philani:	Yes, if you give someone money they might just buy *gavine* [homemade cane spirits]—and that is making the problem worse.

Sipho read from Isaiah 58 about the fasting that God wants.

Sipho:	The gospel must do away with injustice and the yoke of oppression, and it also means giving food, shelter and clothes.
Sandile:	This is the practical gospel.
Philani:	Is this the first step?
Sara:	A tramp asked me for money for tea, so I offered to go with him and buy him some tea and food—but he refused, he just wanted money.
Sandile:	It doesn't always help to give people money.
Sipho:	You must give them help in the right way.
Sandile:	It is like the Red Cross and St Johns during the floods in 1987. The help which they gave was useless—it was worth nothing.
Mbuso:	But half a loaf is better than nothing.

Sipho: Sometimes help can be harmful.

Mbuso: They should have made the people work, so that they felt as though they owned it.

Sandile: What about the old people who couldn't work? They didn't give shelter to Zwane [an old man whose house had been destroyed]. They gave him building materials, but they didn't help him build a house. That material was useless to him.

Mbuso: The Ilimo Project helped Zwane [by organizing the community to help with the construction of his house], who was being helped by the Red Cross.

Sandile: How would he have a house without Ilimo? Other people have material but no houses.

Mbuso: It is the system that is different.

Sipho: Sometimes giving can be harmful. In Isaiah it says we should help with what is needed.

Sandile: The Red Cross made Zwane feel more pain. They gave him building materials but he couldn't use them. They didn't help in a way that he really needed.

Sipho: Preaching the good news is important, and so is sharing things with people in need. But we also need to change the injustice that is causing the poverty.

Mbuso: You know the white church working in Amawoti—they have taxis, a shop, and they sell blocks. Gregory [the pastor] is making money from working in Amawoti. Is he sharing with the poor?

Philani: Why do you give something to the poor? What do you benefit?

Phumzile: St Johns benefits by getting a good reputation by advertising what they do in Amawoti.

Philani: I was thinking more about how individuals benefit.

Sandile: People may respect you if you give them something.

Sipho: What do you think, Philani?

Philani: I don't know.

Sipho: The reason for giving is to help the person in need—it is not for yourself.

Philani: There is a passage in the Bible saying that you should give quietly, not to get attention for yourself.

Mbuso: It's like throwing a stone into the river at the beginning and it becomes bigger and bigger until it gets to the mouth.

Sandile: So you give in order to be given.

Philani: If you give, God will also give back to you.

Sipho: We should give because people are in need, not because we are going to benefit. God will provide for what we need.

The group discussion ended by the group making a poster in which they compiled the most important things that they had learnt. This was put up on the wall of the Ilimo Project office.

[The poster]
Jesus came
- for the rejected and neglected people

He came with the answer to their problem
God's kingdom
- is where God's project is carried out:
    - good news is coming to the poor
    - the oppressed are liberated
- is people who build people

In Amawoti, we see God's kingdom when:
- the community is organized
    - they use good ways to meet needs
- they make changes
- leaders are servants of the community[2]

---

2.   Philpott, *Jesus Is Tricky*, pp. 148-57.

8 |

Remembering Rizpah:
Rizpah 'Re-membering' Us

In this, the concluding chapter, there are echoes and resonances with what has gone before. Working from an actual reading of a biblical text, I wish to draw together some of the things I think we can learn from reading in this way. A reading of 2 Sam. 21.1-14 shapes the chapter, but this reading will also be allowed to resonate with and elaborate the other readings encountered in earlier chapters.

I came across Rizpah while teaching a course on the 'Succession Narrative' (2 Sam. 9–1 Kgs 2). While for most commentators she is a prop in someone else's plot,[1] I recognized her as someone with a story of her own. She reminded me of others I had seen sitting silently. And so it was with excitement and expectation that I entered my class on the day we were to discuss this text.

We had by this time been reading 2 Samuel together regularly and the class was familiar with our literary approach. I allowed the class to guide our reading, but I watched closely, waiting for Rizpah to speak. It was with growing disappointment that I realized that she would not speak. David, the Gibeonites, and even the almost absent Saul were given voice, but not Rizpah.

---

1.   Some exceptions, where Rizpah briefly tells something of her own story, are Janice Nunnally-Cox, *Fore-mothers: Women of the Bible* (New York: Seabury, 1981), pp. 79-81; Glen V. Wiberg, 'The Liturgy of Rizpah', *Covenant Quarterly* 45 (1987), pp. 107-11; Calvin Cook, 'Rizpah's Vigil: Stabat Mater', *Journal of Theology for Southern Africa* 67 (1989), pp. 77-78; Miriam Therese Winter, *Woman Witness: A Feminist Lectionary and Psalter: Women of the Hebrew Scriptures, Part One* (New York: Crossroad, 1992), pp. 170-71; Joyce Hollyday, *Clothed with the Sun: Biblical Women, Social Justice, and Us* (Louisville, KY: Westminster/John Knox Press, 1994), pp. 126-29.

The class consists almost entirely of black South Africans, the majority of whom come from poor and marginalized communities. But less than a quarter of the class are women, and they did not speak at all. The male discussion concentrated on the characters of David and the Gibeonites, and their stories and theologies were closely examined. Even when I intervened and said, 'We have heard the stories and theologies of the fathers, but what about the stories and theologies of the mothers?!', the women remained silent still, quietly shaking their heads. I know now that they were sitting silently in solidarity with Rizpah.

I have used this text often since in various contexts, some of them safe sequested sites in which women and some men read with Rizpah. This paper presents a communal reading of 2 Sam. 21.1-14. The reading emerges from a series of contextual Bible Studies in various communities in South Africa. All of these Bible Studies were facilitated by me, and so were shaped by my interpretative and social interests. However, as I have repeatedly emphasized, the contextual Bible Study process is an enabling process in which 'called' trained readers read the Bible 'with' untrained ordinary 'readers' from poor and marginalized communities. Therefore, the concerns, questions, needs and experiences of these other 'readers' have substantially shaped the reading. But my hand is the final hand, and so the reading in its final form is my production.

As facilitator of the reading process I offered and enabled a variety of questions from literary, postmodern/poststructuralist, and liberationist perspectives. So, for example, questions on the limits of the text enabled readers to recognize 2 Sam. 21.1-14 as a literary unit, and questions about the characters in the text encouraged a close and careful reading of the text, focusing on the text itself rather than on their remembered reconstructions of the larger story of David. I also offered questions that probed the gaps, juxtapositions, presences/absences, and ambiguities within the text, and in so doing provided resources for a postmodern/poststructuralist reading. Ordinary 'readers', of course, brought their many resources for reading and 're-membering'. They also brought their experiences of marginalization and poverty to the reading process. Emancipatory concerns and commitments shaped the entire process.

The reading of this text offered here is a communal product which draws deeply on the readings of those who know Rizpah better than I do. Rizpah has come to live with us and we have become her people. With her we have begun to recognize, recover, revive and arouse the subjugated discourses and hidden transcripts of the biblical tradition and make them our own. We have also come to articulate and own the incipient and inchoate readings and theologies that we live by. I have seen Rizpah often before, although I did not know her name, but I have only begun to hear her story by reading with others who know her.

In each of the various groups in which this text was read a similar reading framework was used. This framework is an expression of the commitments of the contextual Bible study process, which include commitments to read the Bible from the perspective of the organized poor and marginalized, to read the Bible communally, to read the Bible critically, and to read the Bible for social and individual transformation.[2] In reading 2 Sam. 21.1-14 we used the following questions.

1. Read this passage together and retell the story to each other.

2. What is this passage about? Share your responses in the group.

3. Who are the major characters in the story and what do we know about them?

4. What is David's theology in this text?
   What is the Gibeonites' theology?
   What is Rizpah's theology?
   What is the narrator's theology?

5. Which theology do you identify with, and why?

6. What challenges does this text pose for the church in South Africa today?

Questions 1, 2, 5 and 6 focus on community consciousness, concentrating on forms of engagement with the text and each other. Questions 3 and 4 focus on critical consciousness, concentrating on forms of critical distance generated by a close and careful reading of the text. Our close and careful reading used

---

2. West, *Biblical Hermeneutics*, pp. 216-38.

many translations of the Bible in many languages, but only I read the Hebrew text.

Not everybody read with Rizpah, and so our reading is a marginal reading which is located among other contending readings. Most readers initially read with David, a godly character whom they know and trust from their readings of other texts. And this story seemed to confirm their confidence in David; his response to the famine is to 'seek the face of God' (1a). But then some readers pointed out that the famine was already in its third year (1a). Why had it taken David so long to 'seek the face of God'? Did this suggest that David was not as close to God as he should have been? Unease with David grew when he did not immediately choose the first of the options offered by the Gibeonites: restitution through 'silver or gold' (4a). How could he agree to restitution through blood?[3] Did this mean that David was not as close to his people as he should have been? Or did it indicate, as some argued, that David was being particularly sensitive to the power dynamics implicit in the situation; namely, that because the Gibeonites were a marginalized community their initial response was one of deference (4a). Being aware of relations of power, David gave them the space to articulate their real request by making it clear to them that he was giving them the right to decide: 'What do *you say* that I should do for you?' (4b).

Perhaps, some said, David was even using this opportunity to rid himself of potential opposition from Saul's house. David might have been using the Gibeonites, pushing them to execute his own political interests. This line of reasoning appeared to be supported, some readers argued, by the repeated presence of Saul and his 'house' in the story. Participants pointed to the reference to Saul's '*house* of blood' (1b), the Gibeonites' reminder that Saul was 'the chosen of God' (6a),[4] and also drew on what they knew about the tensions between David and Saul from other texts. This would explain, they suggested, why David did not take up the opportunity provided by the first response of the Gibeonites to offer monetary compensation (4a). Some went further and argued

3.   'Restitution' is an important concept in South Africa at this time, although it carries several senses. As participants used different languages, I have used a term that we all identify with in some way.

4.   This phrase is included in most translations.

that David's refusal to take this option and the repetition of the question allowed or even prompted the Gibeonites to make the decision they did. They understood the illocutionary force—the unspoken intent—of David's repeated question: David wanted Saul's family to be eliminated as a potential threat to his throne. Realizing this, the Gibeonites obliged, either for reasons of their own or because they had little option given their position. In their initial request the option of 'silver or gold' is grammatically linked to 'Saul and his family' and the option of 'putting to death' to 'anyone in Israel' (4a), but when David asks the second time, the object of the killing is clear, though Saul is not mentioned by name (5-6a).

None of the readers much liked the idea of David using the Gibeonites for his own ends; in fact, those reading with David became more and more uncomfortable with the David of this story.[5] But those reading with the Gibeonites, and this was often the majority, applauded David for doing the appropriate thing. Some form of restitution was clearly implied by God's statement (1b and 2b), and rather than imposing his form of restitution, David asked the Gibeonites for theirs. And when they behaved deferentially, David rightly recognized this as the behaviour of a vulnerable and marginalized group, and so persisted until they felt free to state their preference. David was being remarkably sensitive to the power dynamics in that situation.

These readers went further, arguing that the perspective of the Gibeonites was appropriate and right. Many of these black South African readers were adamant that the Gibeonites were right to demand blood restitution; they too knew what it was to be systematically slaughtered. Blood restitution was an appropriate response to a 'house of blood' (1b) that 'consumed' and 'planned to destroy' (5), particularly when the house in question was the house of the dominant who had used their power to oppress and decimate the vulnerable and marginalized.

This reading led to a heated discussion of capital punishment, which was at that time being debated by the new Constitutional

5.   The chronicler may also have been a reader who was uncomfortable with the David of this story, for he does not include this episode in his retelling of a story of David. I wish to thank Hendrik Bosman for drawing my attention to this omission in Chronicles.

Court in South Africa. Those reading with the Gibeonites insisted that the death penalty must remain and must be reactivated (there being a moratorium at that time), so that those guilty of blood could be appropriately punished. So those reading with the Gibeonites, and those reading with David, sharing as they did a similar theology, felt that David was right when he gave seven relations of Saul into the hands of the Gibeonites (9a) and that the Gibeonites were justified in 'exposing/impaling them' (9a). Further, they showed that their readings were substantiated by the final sentence of the story: 'And God answered prayer for the land after that' (14b). The phrase 'after that', the concluding phrase in Hebrew, clearly referred to the handing over and exposing/hanging/impaling of the family of Saul.

But it was not that clear to all that this phrase should be interpreted in this way. What about Rizpah, some asked, does she not have a part in this story? All the small groups, in working through the questions outlined above, had agreed that Rizpah was one of the major characters, and yet she had played no role in the reading thus far. So the question was pertinent. This question, it proved, probed a deep disquiet in all readers. Rizpah, it slowly began to emerge, had also done the right thing; she had shown honour to the dead.

Reading from a largely African culture, most readers were very uncomfortable with the 'hanging/exposing' (9) of the bodies. Even those who were deeply committed to the perspective of the Gibeonites found this practice difficult to understand. Relatives of the dead must be allowed to bury the dead properly. Disrespect towards the dead was wrong. And so cracks in the dominant reading began to appear.

However, those who read with David found fresh resources for their reading by following this line of thought. While Saul had broken the oath of Israel to the Amorites (2b), David had kept his oath to Jonathan by sparing Mephibosheth (7). This showed that David did honour his relationships, even with those who had a claim to the throne. Moreover, David did honour the dead by bringing the bones of Saul and Jonathan, and the bones of their relatives that had been hung/exposed/impaled, and gave them a proper burial (12-14a). In this respect, then, David did have a different theology to that of the Gibeonites. So, some suggested, the phrase 'after that' probably included not only right restitution but also right burial.

But this reading in turn opened additional fissures and gaps. Those who read with Rizpah, mainly women, located their readings in these places. In providing a proper burial for the dead of Israel, they argued, David had been responding to Rizpah's actions. It was only 'when David was told what Rizpah had done' (11) that he responded appropriately. She had shamed and challenged him by her solidarity with the dead. Verse 10, Rizpah's story, now became foregrounded. How were Rizpah's actions to be interpreted? What was Rizpah saying in her silence?

Among those who read with Rizpah were those who emphasized her silent solidarity with the dead. She was doing what women all over the world do, caring for the dead. And because she was in a marginalized positioned, being a woman and a concubine (11), she was not allowed to care for or bury the dead, including her children, properly, so she stayed in solidarity with them, doing what she could to honour them. Others who read with Rizpah emphasized the 'deafening silence' of her protest. Although silent, by publicly associating herself with the victims of the king's policy, she was engaging in a political act of protest. She was caring for the dead while and because men with power do not care for the living! This was one of those rare moments when the hidden transcript of women's resistance to dominant ideologies and theologies ruptured the public transcript of deference and disguise; what was usually acted and spoken offstage by women, behind the backs of the dominant, now found a public form at centre-stage.

The 'after that' in the final sentence (14b), these readers argued, referred to Rizpah's actions, not David's! God's answering/responding was associated with Rizpah's resistance. This was clear from the narrative where the rains, which were God's response, were directly related to Rizpah's actions (10a). The narrator tells us that Rizpah stayed in solidarity with the dead 'from the beginning of the harvest until the rains poured down on them from the heavens'. The silent cries of Rizpah and the dead were heard by God.

While the narrator seems to suggest, these readers continued, that David might have heard God speak when 'he sought the face of God' (1a), and that he therefore probably had identified the problem as the need to provide some form of restitution for the Gibeonites, the narrator leaves David to find his own solution. God does not speak again. And Rizpah never speaks. But Rizpah's act of solidarity with the victims of the theology of David and the Gibeonites demands a response, from David and from God. God responds first, and the rain falls on Rizpah and the dead (10a). David then also responds, recognizing, we hope, another more accountable, responsible, and compassionate theology.

Finally, it was pointed out, Rizpah was not alone in her solidarity with the dead and her protest. While she was the only one to risk death by rupturing the public transcript of deference and devotion to male leadership, she could not have survived day and night, month after month (10), without the support of her sisters. Perhaps even Saul's daughter, Michal (or Merab),[6] was among those who sustained and strengthened Rizpah. But maybe not. Michal, like the leaders of the Gibeonites, may have actively embraced the dominant theology of retribution and death. Perhaps the 'class' position that came with being a daughter of a king made it difficult to identify with her sisters. Certainly these African readers knew that the class position of white women in South Africa often had this consequence. Their experience too of black (male) leaders, both in civic and church structures, who had lost their community consciousness, who had abandoned *ubuntu*, made the theology of the Gibeonite leaders uncomfortably familiar. And this was the saddest aspect of this story for those who read with Rizpah, that marginalized communities of people could embrace a theology of domination and death.

It would be nice to report that this is where our readings rested, that our reading remained with Rizpah. But this reading too was deconstructed. Those who read with David continued to claim textual clues for their reading, contending that the juxtaposition of the final two sentences ('And they did all that the king commanded'; 'And God answered prayer for the land after that' [14]) was clear textual attestation that it was David's actions that elicited God's response. Those reading with the Gibeonites responded to Rizpah by reminding those who read with her that theologies of

---

6. The name of Saul's daughter varies with translations. Some manuscripts read *Merab* and others read *Michal*.

compassion and life had been easily coopted by apartheid, and that such theologies were inadequate if apartheid and its architects were to be completely destroyed.

And so this text remains contested. Perhaps that is the narrator's primary point, that there are contending theologies and theologies of life and death co-exist in our communities. The Bible, like the church, is a site of struggle. But those of us who came to know Rizpah cannot forget her. She is our sister and we are her people. We have been partially constituted by her story; we have also been strengthened in our struggle for survival, liberation and life.

Rizpah reminds us of many important aspects of reading 'otherwise'. First, Rizpah is always and thoroughly represented. She is represented as a character in someone else's story, she is represented as other women read with her, and she is represented again as I re-present these various representations. My presence takes up her place. And yet, the traces of her presence remain, even in her absence, and so I must continue to risk such readings, believing that others who encounter her through my re-presented readings will return to reread this text and in so doing read with her in a way that I perhaps cannot. My preliminary and partial representation of Bible studies where I have read with African women open up potential lines of connection for others to probe more deeply.

For example, two women, Malika Sibeko and Beverley Haddad, having read my re-presented reading of Mk 5.21–6.1,[7] read this text with women in Amawoti, an informal settlement near Durban, and the site of the reading in the previous chapter. In that context they found that women immediately identified with the woman with the haemorrhage. While Jairus's daughter was known in relationship to someone, the woman with the haemorrhage 'had no name, no relationship, and was known only by her illness' (v. 25).[8] The women in Amawoti admired this woman's courage and strength in taking the initiative in her encounter with Jesus,

7. West, 'And the Dumb Do Speak'.

8. Malika Sibeko and Beverley Haddad, 'Reading the Bible "with" Women in Poor and Marginalised Communities in South Africa', *Bulletin for Contextual Theology in Southern Africa and Africa* 3 (1996), pp. 14-18 (15).

as well as her resilience in surviving and hoping throughout the twelve years. She had, they said, 'the right to talk to Jesus'.

A key concern for this group of readers was how to interpret the statement that 'power had gone out from him' (v. 30).

They wrestled together to try to understand what this meant. A debate ensued as to whether this *loss* of power was as a result of him having 'touched a bleeding woman', or whether it was necessary for the power to leave Jesus in order for the woman 'to be made holy'. In other words, did Jesus *lose* power because as a holy teacher he had been contaminated by an unclean woman, or was the power *given* by Jesus to the woman in order for healing and wholeness to occur?[9]

In forming this question these women were focusing on a crucial interpretative issue in their lives. The male leadership of their churches cite this part of the story as the basis for refusal to minister to menstruating women. 'They argue that because power left Jesus when he was touched by a bleeding woman, they too would lose power in their ministry if they touched menstruating women.'[10] However, the women now began to read this story differently, arguing that 'Jesus intended to use his power to empower the disempowered'.[11] Like Rizpah, they began to recognize that there was more than one reading.

When the final question was asked on how the text applied to their situation as women, discussion again centred on this church practice. The women began to openly question and challenge the position of the male leadership of their African Independent Church, who insist 'that they cannot lay hands on a woman when she is menstruating as this will result "in the loss of their power"'. In their type of church, where healing through the laying on of hands is a central practice, this was a significant refusal.

> One women referred to feeling depressed while menstruating when she met other women who were able to receive the laying on of hands. She then felt like a sick person. The women began to voice their anger at the fact they were being denied crucial spiritual resources (laying on of hands, prayer and healing) by the male

---

9.   Sibeko and Haddad, 'Reading the Bible', p. 16.
10. Sibeko and Haddad, 'Reading the Bible', p. 17.
11. Sibeko and Haddad, 'Reading the Bible', p. 17.

leadership who were 'forcing power away from them'. Their personhood was being defined by their state of 'bleeding'. So their 'bleeding' was more important to the church leadership than their spiritual, emotional or physical needs.[12]

A further issue raised by the women of Amawoti 'pertained to the practice of women not being allowed to wear church uniforms during menstruation and thus being forced to sit at the entrance to the worship area'.

> One woman suggested that because this was the case they should not bother to go to church and 'just stay at home'. Another reflected that it did not make sense for her not to put her uniform on when 'her body is the temple of God'. As the temple of God she should not be obliged to participate in the customary purification rite that takes place after seven days. This same reader indignantly noted that the purification ceremony sprinkled holy water on her uniform which she had not worn during menstruation, the church building which she had not entered, and on the congregation with whom she had not associated with. If the ceremony was important for 'purification', why was she who was regarded as unclean not sprinkled with water? This led to a recognition by others that perhaps they had a choice after all. They had the choice to either stay at home or to put on their uniform and go to church![13]

A similar series of concerns emerged when this text was read with African Methodists in the township of Sobantu in Pietermaritzburg. As Methodists, these women are not formally 'confronted with the same oppressive institutional church practice on the menstruation issue as the Amawoti women'. 'Yet', Sibeko and Haddad note,

> some of these women of their own volition choose not to take Holy Communion when they are menstruating. Some Sobantu readers were of the opinion that they did experience 'less power during this time of the month'. When this view was expressed, other readers challenged them strongly 'to sort themselves out'.[14]

For both groups of women, reading with Rizpah enabled the faith of the bleeding woman to become 'the source of faith for these women in their daily lives of cultural, economic and ecclesiastical oppression'. As the facilitators acknowledge,

12. Sibeko and Haddad, 'Reading the Bible', p. 16.
13. Sibeko and Haddad, 'Reading the Bible', p. 16.
14. Sibeko and Haddad, 'Reading the Bible', p. 17.

it would be arrogant to suggest that these women readers have been definitively transformed and empowered through this particular Bible study. There are however, tentative indications that a process of empowerment has begun from their reading of this text. Meeting together as women, to study a text facilitated by women, enabled the readers (and the facilitators!) to explore the oppressive effects of menstruation on their lives, perhaps for the first time publicly in a group. The contextual Bible study process as a process became liberatory as it enabled women to speak unspoken words. This liberating experience led to a request for further Bible studies as the readers yearned for more unspoken possibilities. Empowerment had thus resulted through both the process and the product of the reading.[15]

So, secondly, I must continue to risk such readings because I need to be partially constituted by Rizpah and those women who have read with her. My becoming self requires that the traces of her story be put next to mine,[16] enabling me to become more whole. 'Reading with' redeems me, and enables me to participate in collaborative work to transform the world with Rizpah and the many millions who stand in continuity with her struggle for survival, liberation and life. Evelyn-Tashi, in Alice Walker's *Possessing the Secret of Joy*, who is about to be executed for killing M'Lissa, a *tsunga* (the woman who circumcises young women in an Olinka community), is one example:

> Every day now, down below my window in the street, there are demonstrations. I can not see them, but the babble of voices rises up the wall of the prison and pours right through the iron bars.
> What I am really hearing, says Olivia, is the cultural fundamentalists and Moslem fanatics attacking women who've traveled from all parts of the country to place offerings beneath the shrubbery that is just below and around the corner from my view. The women bring wildflowers, herbs, seeds, beads, ears of corn, anything they can claim as their own and that they can spare. They are mostly quiet. Sometimes they sing. It is when they sing that the men attack, even though the only song they all know and can sing together is the national anthem. They hit the women with their fists. They kick them. They swing at them with clubs, bruising the women's skins and breaking bones. The women do not fight back but scatter like hens; huddling in the doorways of shops up and

---

15. Sibeko and Haddad, 'Reading the Bible', pp. 17-18.
16. There is a similar line in Toni Morrison, *Jazz* (New York: Plume, 1993).

down the street, until the shopkeepers sweep them back into the
street with their brooms.

On the day I was sentenced to death the men did not bother the
women, who, according to Olivia, simply sat, spent, hidden as
much as they could be, at the base of the dusty shrubbery. They did
not talk. They did not eat. They did not sing. I had not realized,
before she told me of their dejection, how used I had become to
their clamor. Even with my family beside me, cushioning the blow
of the death sentence, without the noise of the battle from the
street I felt alone.

But then, the next day, the singing began again, low and mourn-
ful, and the sound of sticks against flesh.[17]

Third, reading with Rizpah reminds us that the process of 'reading with', in which socially engaged biblical scholars and ordinary
'readers' of the Bible in poor and marginalized communities read
together with vigilantly foregrounded subject positions, is in itself
no guarantee of an uncontested reading. Rizpah, and the subordinate groups she represents, tend to disguise their resistance and
defiance, and so finding their texts and tales is far from easy. This,
of course, is quite deliberate. What makes our attempts to read
with them more difficult is that dominant texts not only subjugate
and marginalize the tales and texts of the dominated, they also
subsume and coopt them. This is particularly so with text. Oral
culture is more difficult to coopt, and so remains the prefered
medium of subordinate groups. When such tales are taken up
as text, whether in an attempt to coopt and so silence them, or
whether unsuspectingly because of their disguise, they become
more difficult to detect. So, reading with Rizpah reminds us to
listen for other voices in the text, and that there is always more
than one voice to read with.

But, Rizpah would want to remind us, there are reading resources within biblical studies and 're-membering' resources in
the resisting communities of others that enable us to attempt to
track and trace the boundaries of the text in search of her tale of
terror and resistance. We, socially engaged biblical scholars, have
reading resources for 'a more nuanced and literary reading' of
the public transcript, provided we read with those who have the
other 'reading' resources we require for this task. So the fourth

17. Alice Walker, *Possessing the Secret of Joy* (London: Vintage, 1993), pp.
183-84.

thing that reading with Rizpah reminds us of is that we have resources for participating in the construction of power/knowledge, to use Foucault's formulation.[18] In offering our critical reading resources to ordinary 'readers' we provide them with additional critical resources to construct knowledge through their readings of the Bible and so to have potential forms of power in their interactions with dominant forces in the church and society. Knowledge is power, and to have knowledge of the Bible offers them a place in the space that is usually taken up by others like us.[19]

A fifth, related, feature Rizpah reminds us of is that reading methodologies are there to be made use of. Various modes of reading are there to serve us, not us them. While ordinary 'readers' are less squeamish about how they use reading resources than biblical scholars, we too are aware of the eclectic and strategic reading moves we (often?) make. The ordinary 'readers' we socially engaged biblical scholars read with, teach us, as does Rizpah, that this is okay. We will only hear the silences of the text when we abandon notions of methodological purity and begin to make use of multiple methodologies, whether from the scholarly store or from the provisions of local communities of the poor and marginalized—when we use whatever means we have in hand 'to free the meanings struggling to be freed, even if those means reside outside the bounds of methodological conventionality, outside the bounds of the hegemonic OK'.[20]

A sixth, and again related, feature that reading with Rizpah reminds us of is not readily discernible in the reading presented above, but sits behind it. The Bible studies that produced this reading are themselves sites 'in which communicative practice engenders democratic values through the enhancement of communicative competence [in Habermas's sense of these terms]'.[21] Contextual Bible study, where forms of community consciousness

---

18. Foucault, *Power/knowledge*.

19. See Martin Mandew, 'Power and Empowerment: Religious Imagination and the Life of a Local Base Ecclesial Community' (unpublished MA Thesis, University of Natal, 1993), pp. 99-101.

20. Hendricks, 'Guerrilla Exegesis', p. 79.

21. Cochrane, 'Circles of Dignity', p. 115.

and critical consciousness find moments of intersection and transaction, provides resources and a place where members of poor
and marginalized communities can meet, communicate, construct
knowledge and coordinate their actions. The contextual Bible
study process enables what is inchoate and incipient to be articulated, owned, and acted on. As I have indicated, part of my purpose in presenting readings of particular communities, re-presented as they are, is to bring a wider audience directly to the
challenge confronting all of us that the communicative activity of
poor and marginalized local communities represent. Affirming
the particularity and partiality of these readings, produced as they
are in real local struggles for survival, liberation, and life, against
tangible local forces of dehumanization, destruction, death, is
also a part of my purpose. But while Rizpah does remind us of
these things, as we have seen, she also reminds us of *the process* that
enables the articulation and that produced the particular
readings; so clarifying and proclaiming *process* is a considerable
part of my purpose and a substantial challenge to the socially
engaged biblical scholar.[22]

Reading with Rizpah reminds us, seventhly, that there are other
questions, the questions of others, which we can bring to our
research as biblical scholars. By only talking among ourselves, we
biblical scholars curtail the questions that can be brought to the
task of biblical studies. Through the process of reading with
Rizpah we encounter new questions. The reading of Mk 5.21–6.1
recounted above is an example in which other, sometimes strange,
questions are asked of the text. The reading of the Joseph story
outlined in an earlier chapter is another example. In reading that
story in local communities of the poor and marginalized, using
Azaria Mbatha's woodcut as a resource, we recognized that we
could draw on other African resources and questions to recover
aspects of the story which are only partially present in Mbatha's
reading. African women readers began to probe for ways of
uncovering the only partially told story of the women characters.
Although the story appears to be about a father and his sons, the
movement of the plot is really determined by the respective relationships between the wives (Leah, Rachel, Bilhah and Zilpah)

22. I am drawing here on the insightful analysis of Cochrane, 'Circles of
Dignity', p. 56.

and their husband (Jacob) and between these mothers and their sons. African readers, they recognized, had resources in their own traditions and cultures which could uncover and recover this matrilineal presence and power.

In probing the presence and power of women in the story we could draw on the distinction in Nguni culture between *indlovukazi* ('first wife': Leah), *inthandokazi* ('favourite wife': Rachel), and *isancinza* ('helper to the wife': Bilhah and Zilpah) as a resource for exploring the relationships between the women and their husband and their respective sons.[23] That Reuben and Judah are the sons of *indlovukazi*, who is also the sister of *inthandokazi*, may help us to understand their attempts to spare his life (37.21-22, 26-27), and later in the story Judah's intervention on behalf of Benjamin (44.18-34). Joseph's demand that Benjamin be brought to Egypt is clearly connected to him being 'his own mother's son' (43.29).

We might not always find the resources and experiences of ordinary 'readers', and the questions their experiences and resources generate, appropriate, but perhaps through the process of 'reading with' in which we become partially constituted—in which we become 'other'—we can begin to hear beyond the boundaries and din of our difference that there are questions other than our own.

The borders reading with Rizpah bids us to cross may remake us so that we are unable to return to where we have come from; we will have been partially constituted by others. This is the final effect of reading with Rizpah, to realize that readings have effects. Readings matter, they have social effects. To read with the victims of dominant readings is profoundly transforming. To feel the effects of received readings and to be touched by the devastation they bring as we read with others, particularly if we have played a part in generating these readings, will change us forever.[24] But enough of talk, it is after all our work with others that transforms

23. See West, 'Difference and Dialogue'.

24. Jim Perkinson makes a similar point when he argues that knowledge, both social and self-knowledge, is possible for an oppressor 'only as the growing effect of a "dislocation" into concrete, politically committed relationship to (on their own terms) those who are oppressed'; Jim Perkinson, 'On Being "Surged" against: White (Post-) Supremacist Eisegesis as Response to Insurgent African American Exegesis', *Koinonia* 7 (1995), pp. 43-58.

us and our world—and 'reading with' is only one aspect of working with the other—so it is time once again to stand with Rizpah as she fends off the forces of death and destruction in her struggle for survival, liberation and life.

Bibliography

Abrams, M.H., *The Mirror and the Lamp: Romantic Theory and the Critical Tradition* (New York: W.W. Norton, 1958).

Anderson, Janice Capel, and Jeffrey L. Staley (eds.), *Taking It Personally: Autobiographical Biblical Criticism* (Semeia, 72; Atlanta: Scholars Press, 1995).

Appiah-Kubi, Kofi, 'Indigenous African Christian Churches: Sins of Authenticity', in Kofi Appiah-Kubi and Sergio Torres (eds.), *African Theology en Route: Papers from the Pan-African Conference of Third World Theologians, Accra, December 17–23, 1977* (Maryknoll, NY: Orbis Books, 1977), pp. 117-25.

Arnott, Jill, 'French Feminism in a South African Frame? Gayatri Spivak and the Problem of "Representation" in South African Feminism', in M.J. Daymond (ed.), *South African Feminisms: Writing, Theory, and Criticism, 1990–1994* (New York and London: Garland, 1996), pp. 77-89.

Attwell, David, 'Introduction', *Current Writing* 5 (1993), pp. 1-6.

Balcomb, Anthony O., 'Modernity and the African Experience', *Bulletin for Contextual Theology in Southern Africa and Africa* 3 (1996), pp. 12-20.

Bal, Mieke, *Death and Dissymmetry: The Politics of Coherence in the Book of Judges* (Chicago: University of Chicago Press, 1988).

Banana, Canaan S., 'The Case for a New Bible', in Isabel Mukonyora, James L. Cox and Frans J. Verstraelen (eds.), *'Rewriting' the Bible: The Real Issues: Perspectives from within Biblical and Religious Studies in Zimbabwe* (Gweru: Mambo Press, 1993), pp. 17-32.

Barrett, David B., *Schism and Renewal in Africa: An Analysis of Six Thousand Contemporary Religious Movements* (Nairobi: Oxford University Press, 1968).

Barr, James, *Explorations in Theology. VII. The Scope and Authority of the Bible* (London: SCM Press, 1980).

Barton, John, *Reading the Old Testament: Method in Biblical Study* (London: Darton, Longman & Todd, 1984).

Bediako, Kwame, 'Epilogue', in Ype Schaaf, *On their Way Rejoicing: The History and Role of the Bible in Africa* (Carlisle: Paternoster Press, 1994), pp. 241-54.

—'Translatability: Reading the Christian Scriptures in African Languages' (unpublished paper).

Bledstein, A.J., 'Binder, Trickster, Heel and Hairy-man: Re-reading Genesis 27 as a Trickster Tale Told by a Woman' (unpublished paper, SBL, 1991).

Boff, Clodovis, *Theology and Praxis: Epistemological Foundations* (Maryknoll, NY: Orbis Books, 1987).

Brett, Mark G., 'Four or Five Things to Do with Texts: A Taxonomy of Interpretative Interests', in David J.A. Clines, Stephen E. Fowl and Stanley E. Porter (eds.), *The Bible in Three Dimensions: Essays in Celebration of Forty Years of Biblical Studies in the University of Sheffield* (JSOTSup, 87; Sheffield: Sheffield Academic Press, 1990), pp. 357-77.

—'The Political Ethics of Postmodern Allegory', in M. Daniel Carroll R., David J.A. Clines and Philip R. Davies (eds.), *The Bible in Human Society: Essays in Honour of John Rogerson* (JSOTSup, 200; Sheffield: Sheffield Academic Press, 1995), pp. 67-86.

—'Interpreting Ethnicity', in Mark G. Brett (ed.), *Ethnicity and the Bible* (Leiden: E.J. Brill, 1996), pp. 3-22.

Cady, Linell E., 'Hermeneutics and Tradition: The Role of the Past in Jurisprudence and Theology', *Harvard Theological Journal* 79 (1986), pp. 439-63.

Cochrane, James R., 'Already, But Not Yet: Programmatic Notes for a Theology of Work', in J.R. Cochrane and G.O. West, *The Threefold Cord: Theology, Work and Labour* (Pietermaritzburg: Cluster Publications, 1991), pp. 177-89.

—'Circles of Dignity: Incipient Theologies and the Integrity of Faith in a Postcolonial Era' (unpublished manuscript).

Collins, Patricia Hill, *Black Feminist Thought: Knowledge, Consciousness, and the Politics of Empowerment* (London: HarperCollins, 1990).

Comaroff, Jean, *Body of Power, Spirit of Resistance: The Culture and History of a South African People* (Chicago: University of Chicago Press, 1985).

Comaroff, Jean, and John Comaroff, *Of Revelation and Revolution: Christianity, Colonialism, and Consciousness in South Africa* (Chicago: University of Chicago Press, 1991).

—*Modernity and its Malcontents: Ritual and Power in Postcolonial Africa* (Chicago: University of Chicago Press, 1993).

Cook, Calvin, 'Rizpah's Vigil: Stabat Mater', *Journal of Theology for Southern Africa* 67 (1989), pp. 77-78.

Cragg, Kenneth, *Christianity in World Perspective* (London: Lutterworth Press, 1968).

Croatto, Jóse Severino, *Biblical Hermeneutics: Toward a Theory of Reading as the Production of Meaning* (Maryknoll, NY: Orbis Books, 1987).

Daly, Mary, *Gynecology: The Metaethics of Radical Feminism* (Boston: Beacon Press, 1978).

De Oliveira, Rosangela Soares, 'Feminist Theology in Brazil', in Ofelia Ortega (ed.), *Women's Vision: Theological Reflection, Celebration, Action* (Geneva: World Council of Churches, 1995), pp. 65-76.

Draper, Jonathan A., and Gerald O. West, 'Anglicans and Scripture in South Africa', in Frank England and Torquil J.M. Paterson (eds.), *Bounty in Bondage* (Johannesburg: Ravan, 1989), pp. 30-52.

—' "Go Sell All You Have…" (Mark 10.17-30)', *Journal of Theology for Southern Africa* 79 (1992), pp. 63-69.

—'Wandering Radicalism or Purposeful Activity? Jesus and the Sending of Messengers in Mark 6.6-56', *Neotestamentica* 29 (1995), pp. 187-207.

—'Confessional Western Text-Centred Biblical Interpretation and an Oral or Residual-Oral Context', *Semeia* 73 (1996), pp. 59-77.

Eagleton, Terry, *The Function of Criticism: from the Spectator to Post-Structuralism* (London: Verso, 1984).

—'Reception Theory', in P. Barry (ed.), *Issues in Contemporary Critical Theory* (London: Macmillan, 1989), pp. 119-27.

Ellsworth, Elizabeth, 'Why Doesn't This Feel Empowering? Working through the Repressive Myths of Critical Pedagogy', *Harvard Educational Review* 59 (1989), pp. 297-324.

Foucault, Michel, *Power/Knowledge: Selected Writings and Other Interviews* (New York: Pantheon, 1980).

Fowl, Stephen E., 'The Ethics of Interpretation or What's Left Over after the Elimination of Meaning', in David J.A. Clines, Stephen E. Fowl and Stanley E. Porter (eds.), *The Bible in Three Dimensions: Essays in Celebration of Forty Years of Biblical Studies in the University of Sheffield* (JSOTSup, 87; Sheffield: Sheffield Academic Press, 1990), pp. 379-98.

—'Texts Don't Have Ideologies', *Biblical Interpretation* 3 (1995), pp. 15-34.

Freire, Paulo, *Pedagogy of the Oppressed* (New York: Continuum, 1970).

Frostin, Per, *Liberation Theology in Tanzania and South Africa: A First World Interpretation* (Lund: Lund University Press, 1988).

Fulkerson, Mary McClintock, *Changing the Subject: Women's Discourses and Feminist Theology* (Minneapolis: Fortress Press, 1994).

Gadamer, Hans-Georg, *Truth and Method* (New York: Seabury, 1975).

Getui, Mary N., 'The Bible as a Tool for Ecumenism', in Hannah W. Kinoti and John M. Waliggo (eds.), *The Bible in African Christianity* (Nairobi: Acton Publishers), pp. 86-98.

Giroux, H.A., 'Introduction', in Paulo Freire, *The Politics of Education* (London: Macmillan, 1985), pp. xi-xxv.

Goss, Jasper, 'Postcolonialism: Subverting Whose Empire?', *Third World Quarterly* 17 (1996), pp. 239-50.

Gottwald, Norman K., *The Tribes of Yahweh: A Sociology of the Religion of Liberated Israel, 1250–1050 BC* (Maryknoll, NY: Orbis Books, 1979).

—*The Hebrew Bible: A Socio-literary Introduction* (Philadelphia: Fortress Press, 1985).

Gramsci, Antonio, *Selections from the Prison Notebooks* (ed. and trans. Quintin Hoare and Geoffrey Nowel Smith; London: Lawrence and Wishart, 1971).

Gutiérrez, Gustavo, *A Theology of Liberation: History, Politics and Salvation* (London: SCM Press, 1974).

Haddad, Beverley, 'En-gendering a Theology of Development: Raising Some Preliminary Issues', in Leonard Hulley, Louise Kretzschmar and Luke Lungile Pato (eds.), *Archbishop Tutu: Prophetic Witness in South Africa* (Cape Town: Human and Rousseau, 1996), pp. 199-210.

Hendricks, Osayande Obery, 'Guerilla Exegesis: "Struggle" as a Scholarly Vocation: A Postmodern Approach to African-American Interpretation', *Semeia* 72 (1995), pp. 73-90.

Hollyday, Joyce, *Clothed with the Sun: Biblical Women, Social Justice, and Us* (Louisville, KY: Westminster/John Knox Press, 1994).

Horsley, Richard A., *Sociology and the Jesus Movement* (New York: Crossroad, 1989).

Hutcheon, Linda, 'Circling the Downspout of Empire', in Ian Adam and Helen Tiffin (eds.), *Past the Last Post: Theorizing Post-colonialism and Post-modernism* (New York: Harvester, 1991), pp. 167-89.

ICT Church and Labour Project Research Group, 'Workers, the Church and the Alienation of Religious Life', in J.R. Cochrane and G.O. West, *The Threefold Cord: Theology, Work and Labour* (Pietermaritzburg: Cluster Publications, 1991), pp. 253-75.

Isichei, Elizabeth, *A History of Christianity in Africa: From Antiquity to the Present* (Grand Rapids: Eerdmans, 1995).

Jobling, David, 'Writing the Wrongs of the World: The Deconstruction of the Biblical Text in the Context of Liberation Theologies', *Semeia* 51 (1990), pp. 81-118.

Kinoti, Hannah W., and John M. Waliggo (eds.), *The Bible in African Christianity: Essays in Biblical Theology* (Nairobi: Acton Publishers, 1997).

Kirby, Kathleen M., 'Thinking through the Boundary: The Politics of Location, Subjects, and Space', *Boundary 2* 20 (1993), pp. 173-89.

Kock, Leon de, 'Postcolonial Analysis and the Question of Critical Disablement', *Current Writing* 5 (1993), pp. 44-69.

Lategan, Bernard C., 'Current Issues in the Hermeneutic Debate', *Neotestamentica* 8 (1984), pp. 1-17.

Long, Timothy M.S., 'A Real Reader Reading *Revelation*', *Semeia* 73 (1996), pp. 79-107.

Lorde, Audre, *Sister Outsider* (New York: The Crossing Press, 1984).

Lyotard, Jean-François, *The Postmodern Condition: A Report on Knowledge* (Minneapolis: University of Minnesota Press, 1984).

Mailloux, S., 'Rhetorical Hermeneutics', *Critical Inquiry* 11 (1985), pp. 620-41.

Maluleke 1996, Tinyiko Sam, 'Black and African Theologies in the New World Order', *Journal of Theology for Southern Africa* 96 (1996), pp. 3-19.

Mandew, Martin, 'Power and Empowerment: Religious Imagination and the Life of the Local Base Ecclesial Community' (unpublished MA Thesis, University of Natal, 1993).

Marais, Michael, 'Reading Postmodernism(s): A Review Essay', *Current Writing* 5 (1993), pp. 134-41.

Martin, Clarice J., 'The *Haustafeln* (Household Codes) in African American Biblical Interpretation: "Free Slaves" and "Subordinate Women"', in Cain Hope Felder (ed.), *Stony the Road We Trod: African American Biblical Interpretation* (Minneapolis: Fortress Press, 1991), pp. 206-31.

Masipa, Lekoapa P., 'The Use of the Bible in Black Theology with Reference to the Exodus Story' (MTh. Thesis, University of Natal, 1997).

Mbatha, Azaria, *Im Herzen des Tigers: In the Heart of the Tiger*. Text by Werner Eichel. (Wuppertal: Peter Hammer Verlag, 1986).

Mbiti, John S., 'The Biblical Basis for Present Trends in African Theology', in Appiah-Kubi and Torres (eds.), *African Theology en Route*, pp. 83-94.

McKnight, Edgar V., *The Bible and the Reader: An Introduction to Literary Criticism* (Philadelphia: Fortress Press, 1985).

Metz, Johann Baptist, *Faith in History and Society: Toward a Practical Fundamental Theology* (London: Burns and Oates, 1980).

Meyers, Carol, *Discovering Eve: Ancient Israelite Women in Context* (Oxford: Oxford University Press, 1988).

Mofokeng, Takatso, 'Black Christians, the Bible and Liberation' *The Journal of Black Theology* 2 (1988), pp. 34-42.

Moore, Stephen D., 'Doing Gospel Criticism as/with a "Reader"', *Biblical Theology Bulletin* 19 (1989), pp. 85-93.

—*Literary Criticism and the Gospels Today: Landmarks, Fault Lines, Time Zones* (New Haven: Yale University Press, 1989).

—'True Confessions and Weird Obsessions: Autobiographical Interventions in Literary and Biblical Studies', *Semeia* 72 (1995), pp. 19-50.

Morrison, Toni, *Jazz* (New York: Plume, 1993).

Mosala, Itumeleng J., 'The Use of the Bible in Black Theology', in Itumeleng J. Mosala and Bhuti Tlhagale (eds.), *The Unquestionable Right to Be Free* (Johannesburg: Skotaville, 1986), pp. 175-99.

—*Biblical Hermeneutics and Black Theology in South Africa* (Grand Rapids: Eerdmans, 1989).

—'Race, Class, and Gender as Hermeneutical Factors in the African Independent Churches' Appropriation of the Bible', *Semeia* 73 (1996), pp. 43-57.

Ndungu, Nahashon, 'The Bible in an African Independent Church', in Hannah W. Kinoti and John M. Waliggo (eds.), *The Bible in African Christianity* (Nairobi: Acton Publishers, 1997), pp. 58-67.

Nolan, Albert, *Jesus before Christianity: The Gospel of Liberation* (Cape Town: David Philip, 1986).

—*God in South Africa: The Challenge of the Gospel* (Cape Town: David Philip, 1988).

—'Work, the Bible, Workers, and Theologians: Element's of a Workers' Theology', *Semeia* 73 (1996), pp. 213-20.

Nthamburi, Zablon, and Douglas Waruta, 'Biblical Hermeneutics in African Instituted Churches', in Hannah W. Kinoti and John M. Waliggo (eds.), *The Bible in African Christianity* (Nairobi: Acton Publishers, 1997), pp. 40-57.

Ntreh, Benjamin A., 'Towards an African Biblical Hermeneutic', *Africa Theological Journal* 19, (1990), pp. 247-54.

Nunnally-Cox, Janice, *Fore-mothers: Women of the Bible* (New York: Seabury, 1981).

Patte, Daniel, and Gary Phillips, 'A Fundamental Condition for Ethical Accountability in the Teaching of the Bible by White Male Exegetes: Recovering and Claiming the Specificity of our Perspective', *Scriptura* S9 (1992), pp. 7-28.

Patte, Daniel, *Ethics of Biblical Interpretation: A Reevaluation* (Louisville, KY: Westminster/John Knox Press, 1995).

Perkinson, Jim, 'On Being "Surged" against: White (Post-) Supremacist Eisegesis as Response to Insurgent African American Exegesis', *Koinonia* 7 (1995), pp. 43-58.

Petersen, Robin M., 'Time, Resistance and Reconstruction: Rethinking Kairos Theology' (PhD Disseration, University of Chicago 1995).

Philpott, Graham, *Jesus Is Tricky and God Is Undemocratic: The Kin-dom of God in Amawoti* (Pietermaritzburg: Cluster Publications, 1993).

Philpott, Susan C., Amawoti: 'Responding to the Needs and Rights of People with Disabilities' (MSocSc. Thesis, University of Natal, 1995).

Report of the ISB Biennial Workshop: Women and the Bible in South and Southern Africa (Pietermaritzburg: ISB, 1996).

Rorty, Richard, 'Texts and Lumps', *New Literary History* 17 (1985), pp. 1-16.

Ruether, Rosemary Radford, *Sexism and God-talk: Towards a Feminist Theology* (London: SCM Press, 1983).

Sakenfeld, Katharine Doob, 'Feminist Uses of Biblical Materials', in Letty M. Russel (ed.), *Feminist Interpretations of the Bible* (Philadelphia: Westminster Press, 1985), pp. 55-64.

Sanneh, Lamin, *Translating the Message: The Missionary Impact on Culture* (Maryknoll, NY: Orbis Books, 1989).

Saunders, Cheryl J. (ed.), *Living the Intersection: Womanism and Afrocentrism in Theology* (Minneapolis: Fortress Press, 1995).

Schaaf, Ype, *On their Way Rejoicing: The History and Role of the Bible in Africa* (Carlisle: Paternoster Press, 1994).

Schneiders, Sandra M., 'Feminist Ideology Criticism and Biblical Hermeneutics' *Biblical Theology Bulletin* 19 (1989), pp. 3-10.

Schreiter, Robert J., *Constructing Local Theologies* (Maryknoll, NY: Orbis Books 1985).

Schüssler Fiorenza, E., *In Memory of Her* (London: SCM Press, 1983).

—*Bread Not Stone: The Challenge of Feminist Biblical Interpretation* (Boston: Beacon Press, 1984).

Scott, James C., *Domination and the Arts of Resistance: Hidden Transcipts* (New Haven: Yale University Press, 1990).

Segovia, Fernando F., and Mary Ann Tolbert (eds.), *Reading from This Place: Social Location and Biblical Interpretation in Global Perspective*, II (Minneapolis: Fortress Press, 1995).

Segundo, J.L., 'The Shift within Latin American Theology', *Journal of Theology for Southern Africa* 52 (1985), pp. 17-29.

Sibeko, Malika, and Beverley Haddad, 'Reading the Bible "with" Women in Poor and Marginalised Communities in South Africa', *Bulletin for Contextual Theology in Southern Africa and Africa* 3 (1996), pp. 14-18.

Smith-Christopher, Daniel (ed.), *Text and Experience: Towards a Cultural Exegesis of the Bible* (The Biblical Seminar, 35; Sheffield: Sheffield Academic Press, 1995).

Spivak, Gayatri C., 'Can the Subaltern Speak?', in Gary Nelson and L. Grossberg (eds.), *Marxism and the Interpretation of Culture* (London: Macmillan, 1988), pp. 271-313.

Stine, Philip (ed.), *Bible Translation and the Spread of the Church: The Last 200 Years* (Leiden: E.J. Brill, 1990).

Stout, Jeffery, 'What Is the Meaning of a Text?', *New Literary History* 14 (1982), pp. 1-12.

Sugirtharajah, R.S. (ed.), *Voices from the Margin: Interpreting the Bible in the Third World* (Maryknoll, NY: Orbis Books, 1991).

The Kairos Document: Challenge to the Church (Braamfontein: Skotaville, 1986).

The Road to Damascus: Kairos and Conversion (Johannesburg: Skotaville, 1989).

Tolbert, Mary Ann, 'Reading for Liberation', in Fernando F. Segovia and Mary Ann Tolbert (eds.), *Reading from this Place: Social Location and Biblical Interpretation in the United States*, I (Minneapolis: Fortress Press, 1995), pp. 263-76.

Torres, Sergio, and V. Fabella (eds.), *The Emergent Gospel: Theology from the Underside of History* (Maryknoll, NY: Orbis Books, 1978).

Tracy, David, *Plurality and Ambiguity: Hermeneutics, Religion, Hope* (San Francisco: Harper & Row, 1987).

Trible, Phyllis, *God and the Rhetoric of Sexuality: Overtures to Biblical Theology* (Philadelphia: Fortress Press, 1978)

—*Texts of Terror: Literary-Feminist Readings of Biblical Narratives* (Philadelphia: Fortress Press, 1984).

Truluck, Ann, *No Blood on our Hands* (Pietermaritzburg: Black Sash, 1993).

Ukpong, Justin, 'Port Harcourt Report of the Bible in Africa Project's Findings' (Port Harcourt: Unpublished Report, 1994).

—'Rereading the Bible with African Eyes', *Journal of Theology for Southern Africa* 91 (1995), pp. 3-14.

Waetjen, Herman C., *A Reordering of Power: A Socio-Political Reading of Mark's Gospel* (Minneapolis: Fortress Press, 1989).

Walker, Alice, *Possessing the Secret of Joy* (London: Vintage, 1993).

Watson, Francis, *Text, Church and World Biblical Interpretation in Theological Perspective* (Grand Rapids: Eerdmans, 1994).

Waugh, Patricia, *Practising Postmodernism/Reading Modernism* (London: Edward Arnold, 1992).

Weber, Max, *The Sociology of Religion* (Boston: Beacon Press, 1964).

Weiler, Kathleen, 'Freire and a Feminist Pedagogy of Difference', *Harvard Educational Review* 61 (1991), pp. 449-74.

Welch, Sharon D., *Communities of Resistance and Solidarity: A Feminist Theology of Liberation* (Maryknoll, NY: Orbis Books, 1985).

—*A Feminist Ethic of Risk* (Minneapolis: Fortress Press, 1990).

Wengst, Klaus, *Pax Romana and the Peace of Jesus Christ* (London: SCM Press, 1987).

West, Cornel, 'Afterword: The Politics of American Neo-Pragmatism', in J. Rajchman and C. West (eds.), *Post-Analytic Philosophy* (New York: Columbia University Press, 1985), pp. 270-71.

—*Prophetic Fragments* (Grand Rapids: Eerdmans, 1988).

West, Gerald O., 'The Relationship between Different Modes of Reading and the Ordinary Reader', *Scriptura* S9 (1991), pp. 87-110.

—'The Interface between Trained Readers and Ordinary Readers in Liberation Hermeneutics—A Case Study: Mark 10.17-22', *Neotestamentica* 27 (1993), pp. 165-80.

—*Contextual Bible Study* (Pietermaritzburg: Cluster Publications, 1993).

—'No Integrity Without Contextuality: The Presence of Particularity in Biblical Hermeneutics and Pedagogy', *Scriptura* S11 (1993), pp. 131-46.

—'Difference and Dialogue: Reading the Joseph Story *with* Poor and Marginalized Communities in South Africa', *Biblical Interpretation* 2 (1994), pp. 152-70.

—'And the Dumb Do Speak: Articulating Incipient Readings of the Bible in Marginalised Communities', in John W. Rogerson, Margaret Davies and M. Daniel Carroll R. (eds.), *The Bible in Ethics: The Second Sheffield Colloquium* (JSOTSup, 207; Sheffield: Sheffield Academic Press, 1995), pp. 174-92.

—'Power and Pedagogy in a South African Context: A Case Study in Biblical Studies', *Academic Development* 2 (1996), pp. 47-65.

—'Finding a Place among the Posts for Post-Colonial Criticism in Biblical Studies in South Africa', *Old Testament Essays* 10 (1997), pp. 322-42.

—'Re-membering the Bible in South Africa: Reading Strategies in a Postcolonial Context', *Jian Dao* 8 (1997), pp. 37-62.

West, Gerald O., *Biblical Hermeneutics of Liberation: Modes of Reading the Bible in the South African Context* (Pietermaritzburg: Cluster Publications, 2nd rev. edn, 1995).

Whitelam, W. Keith, *The Invention of Ancient Israel: The Silencing of Palestinian History* (New York: Routledge, 1996).

Wiberg, Glen V., 'The Liturgy of Rizpah', *Covenant Quarterly* 45 (1987), pp. 77-78.

Wilkins, J. (ed.), *Understanding Veritatis Splendor: The Encyclical Letter of Pope John Paul II on the Church's Moral Teaching* (London: SPCK, 1994).

Williams, Dolores, *Sisters in the Wilderness: The Challenge of Womanist God-Talk* (Maryknoll, NY: Orbis Books 1993), pp. 194-99.

Wimbush, Vincent L., 'The Bible and African Americans: An Outline of an Interpretative History', in Cain Hope Felder (ed.), *Stony the Road We Trod: African American Biblical Interpretation* (Minneapolis: Fortress Press, 1991), pp. 81-97.

—'Reading Texts through Worlds, Worlds through Texts', *Semeia* 62 (1993), pp. 129-40.

Winter, Miriam Therese, *Woman Witness: A Feminist Lectionary of the Psalter: Women of the Hebrew Scriptures, Part One* (New York: Crossroad, 1992).

Yorke, Gosnell L.O.R., 'The Bible in the Black Diaspora', in Hannah W. Kinoti and John M. Waliggo (eds.), *The Bible in African Christianity* (Nairobi: Acton Publishers, 1997), pp. 149-52.

INDEXES

INDEX OF BIBLICAL REFERENCES

INDEX OF AUTHORS